The Chronic Silence of Political Parties in End of Life Policymaking in the United States

The Chronic Silence of Political Parties in End of Life Policymaking in the United States

Bianca Easterly

LEXINGTON BOOKS
Lanham • Boulder • New York • London

Published by Lexington Books
An imprint of The Rowman & Littlefield Publishing Group, Inc.
4501 Forbes Boulevard, Suite 200, Lanham, Maryland 20706
www.rowman.com

6 Tinworth Street, London SE11 5AL, United Kingdom

British Library Cataloguing in Publication Information Available

Library of Congress Cataloging-in-Publication Data

Names: Easterly, Bianca, author.
Title: The chronic silence of political parties in end of life policymaking in the United States / Bianca Easterly.
Description: Lanham : Lexington Books, [2019] | Includes bibliographical references and index.
Identifiers: LCCN 2019013144 (print) | LCCN 2019016651 (ebook) | ISBN 9781498556095 (electronic) | ISBN 9781498556088 (cloth)
Subjects: LCSH: Euthanasia—Government policy—United States—History. | Terminal care—Government policy—United States—History. | Right to die—Law and legislation—United States—History. | Medical policy—United States—History. | Political parties—United States—History.
Classification: LCC R726 (ebook) | LCC R726 .E24 2019 (print) | DDC 179.7—dc23
LC record available at https://lccn.loc.gov/2019013144

Contents

List of Tables and Figures vii

Acknowledgments ix

Introduction: The Politics of Death xi

1 Historical Beginnings: The Policy Entrepreneurs of the Early Aid in Dying Movement 1

2 Modern Renewal: State End of Life Policy Adoptions 11

3 Interest Groups 31

4 The Courts 53

5 Health Care Coalitions 77

6 End of Life Polices Today and Tomorrow 91

Bibliography 99

Index 107

About the Author 113

List of Tables and Figures

TABLES

I.1 Physician Prescribed and Administered Aid in Dying States and Countries xvi
2.1 Legislative History of Death with Dignity Laws Adopted by Legislatures or Councils 19
2.2 Legislative History of Death with Dignity Laws Adopted by Ballot Initiative or Referendum 21
2.3 Recent Utilization Demographics 23
4.1 U.S. Physicians Indicted for Murder in *Mercy Killing* Cases 57
5.1 Key Differences Between POLST and Advance Directives 83
6.1 Death with Dignity Legislative Activity 2018/2019 Session as of January 5, 2019 93

FIGURES

5.1 Number of POLST Paradigm Programs Established 1991–2017 84
5.2 POLST Program Designations as of July 6, 2018 86
5.3 Years Before POLST Legislation Adoption 87

Acknowledgments

I am tremendously thankful for the inspiration, support, and words of encouragement I received during the writing of this book and throughout my career. I thank the late Dr. Robert L. Lineberry for always challenging me to "find the politics" in every social problem. I also thank my University of Houston health care policy instructor, Kathleen P. Rubinstein, for fostering my interest in end of life care planning as well as my advisors, Dr. Jennifer Hayes Clark and Dr. Paul Brace for setting an example of excellence as professors, scholars, mentors, and professionals.

I want to express my deepest appreciation for those who directly contributed to the development of the book including research assistance from Shane Benoit, editing services by Kate Epstein, and financial support from Lamar University through a summer research fellowship. I also want to thank Dr. Raymond Tatalovich for his willingness to share his expertise on end of life policies and for believing in this research, and the anonymous reviewer for their careful reading of the manuscript, and many insightful comments and suggestions.

Finally, I must recognize my dedicated friends and family whose love knows no bounds. Special thanks to Shayla Davis who is such a good listener, confidant, and friend. To my brother, Jason L. Easterly, who never misses an opportunity to celebrate my victories but is equally ready to offer an uplifting word or a little humor during my losses. My mother, Liethia Lee Easterly's, personal experiences with death and dying as long-term care nursing director led to many interesting and formative discussions related to this research. Most importantly, I wish to thank my patient husband, Tony, and our incredible son, Maxwell, who play an integral part in making life worth living each day.

Introduction

The Politics of Death

The inclusion of Section 1233, titled "Advance Care Planning Consultation" in the Patient Protection and Affordable Care Act (commonly known as the ACA or "ObamaCare") in the summer of 2009 should have been more of a formality than a political liability.[1] Since the 1990s, Republicans and Democrats have embraced the idea and importance of end of life care planning. The first congressional act related to end of life care occurred in 1990 during the George H. W. Bush administration. The Patient Self-Determination Act (PSDA) requires health care facilities that receive federal funding to inform adult patients about advance directives (e.g., living will, power of attorney, health-care proxy, and DNR [do not resuscitate] order).[2] Ever since, efforts to enhance PSDA's provisions in Congress had involved members of both parties in both chambers.[3] While ACA was a Democrat measure, then Governor Sarah Palin of Alaska had issued a proclamation recognizing Healthcare Decision Day as a statewide initiative to raise public awareness about advance directives and the end of life planning in 2008.[4] Some months later former Republican House Speaker Newt Gingrich publicly praised Gundersen Lutheran Health System of La Crosse, WI for their efforts in promoting advance directives, stating that similar efforts nationwide would save Medicare more than a billion dollars a year.[5]

The legislative intent for Section 1233 was straightforward. House of Representatives member Earl Blumenauer (D-OR) sought to correct what he perceived as a glaring flaw in the current Medicare reimbursement system that did not allow physicians to bill Medicare, the largest insurer of health care provided at the end of life, for voluntary end of life care consultations for all its patients. Research estimates that Medicare spends roughly a quarter of its budget on services for beneficiaries in their last year of life, 40 percent of which is spent in the final thirty days. Medicare reimbursed doctors for almost any medical procedure except time to discuss end of life preferences with their patients, according to the Congressman, and this was "perverse." In fact, in defending the measure Blumenauer suggested it was more radical than it was. The 2003 Medicare Prescription Drug, Improvement, and Modernization Act, which 204 Republican House members and 42 Republican Senators had supported, already provided funding for end of life care and options counseling for terminally ill patients.[6] Section 1233 added reimbursement for physicians conducting end of life conversations with their patients' consent *before* terminal illness.[7] More accurately, Blumenauer explained in an interview that Section 1233 would "give people more control over the care they receive . . . [so that] doctors can have conversations in the normal course of business, as part of our health routine, not as something put off until we are forced to do it."[8]

Blumenauer and the Democratic Party could not have anticipated the swift and immediate changing of the political tide or the distortion of a policy issue that, until that point, had bipartisan consensus. Prominent conservatives and Republicans made Section 1233 their weapon of choice to derail health care reform. Just two days after the bill's introduction, Betsy McCaughey, the former lieutenant governor of New York and a conservative health care commentator, claimed on a conservative radio show that, "Congress would make it mandatory—absolutely require—that every five years people in Medicare have a required counseling session that will tell them how to end their life soon."[9]

Over the next month, conservative radio and television became the primary platforms for opponents to whittle away at the patient-empowering themes associated with end of life counseling to build a mythical threat of medical care denial for seniors. Then on August 7, 2009, Sarah Palin took to Facebook to denounce the fictitious government "death panels." She wrote:

> The America I know and love is not one in which my parents or my baby with Down syndrome will have to stand in front of Obama's death panel.[10]

Chuck Grassley (S-Iowa), a key player in the health care talks as the ranking Republican on the Senate Finance Committee, repeated the lie in a public meeting, suggesting ACA would institute "a government program that determines if you are going to pull the plug on Grandma."[11] A Pew study conducted the same month found that 86 percent of respondents reported hearing the claim that ACA "includes the creation of so called 'death panels' or rationing of care for the critically ill." Among those familiar with the claim, 30 percent believed it.[12] Section 1233 remained in the House version of the Patient Protection and Affordable Care Act, but the Senate intentionally left the section out of the final version that became law in 2010. End of life policymaking would return to the states where the right to die movement began and continues.

Partisan politics and health care reform opposition aside, the myth masterfully played on American culture's uneasy relationship with aging and dying. By 2035, for the first time in the nation's history, people over the age of 65 will outnumber children.[13] Thanks to technological advancements in medicine and science, Americans are living longer, which comes with hefty emotional, ethical, physical, and financial costs. Those who prepare not only reduce the burdens of death on themselves and their loved ones; they also have the luxury of choice. Seven in ten Americans (71 percent) would prefer to end their lives at home, but only about 20 percent of Americans do. The rest expire in acute care hospitals (60 percent) and nursing homes (20 percent).[14] Dying is also expensive.[15] According to a study conducted by the Mount Sinai School of Medicine, out-of-pocket expenses for Medicare recipients during the last five years of life averaged about $39,000 for individuals, $51,000 for couples, and up to $66,000 for people with long-term illness such as Alzheimer's.[16] Retirement funds for most Americans will not come close to what is needed to cover potential out-of-pocket costs and living expenses. The median retirement savings for fifty-five to sixty-four year olds is only $120,000, which is far less than the $1 million experts recommend.[17] Forty percent of US adults do not have any life insurance because of cost and one in five people cannot afford funerals.[18] Overwhelmingly, Americans desire to have their end of life care preferences honored but only a third of the US adults legally document their health care preferences by completing advance directives. Instead of confronting their mortality, most Americans prefer to avoid the topic—and death itself—for as long as they can.[19]

Against the backdrop of the culture of death avoidance exists an ongoing and growing interest in public policies that improve as well as protect end of life choices for the terminally ill. Since 1906, advocates across states have proposed policies that legalize merciful and peaceful death. Until the 1960s, policy initiatives focused exclusively on *euthanasia* (which translates from Greek: *eu* = good, well; *thanatos* = death), the active initiation of death. Over time passive approaches such as the refusal of life-sustaining medical interventions (e.g., mechanical respiration, feeding and hydration) so that death can naturally proceed gained more prominence in the movement. In the 1990s, two policy innovations developed representing the movement's two dimensions—death with dignity and the Physician Orders for Life-Sustaining Treatment (POLST) Paradigm.

DEATH WITH DIGNITY LAWS

The Progressive Era's amalgamation of voluntary (consenting) death and eugenics (which translates from Greek: *eu* = good, well, *genics* = in birth) started with the maltreatment of those deemed "unfit" by tolerating the deliberate killing of infants and adults with disabilities, referred to at the time as *mercy killings,* as well as the enactment of compulsory sterilization laws. By the 1950s, however, the combination of the two movements, which resulted in the Nazi atrocities during World War II, fundamentally buried *euthanasia* reform in the United States. It would revive in the 1970s, using new terms and aligning with the increasingly popular patient-centered approach to medicine. Proponents replaced emotive expressions such as *euthanasia*, *mercy killing*, and *assisted suicide* with terms such as *physician aid in dying* (PAD) and *death with dignity* to emphasize their focus on establishing a right to die. In 1997, Oregon became the first state to adopt a death with dignity law.[20] While the previsions slightly vary from state to state, generally, such laws permit physicians to prescribe patients a lethal dose of barbiturates that patients then take on their own. Six other jurisdictions have adopted similar statutes since—Washington State (2008), Vermont (2013) California (2015), Colorado (2016), the District of Columbia (2016/2017), and Hawaii (2018/2019). Montana effectively permits PAD as well due to the state supreme court's decision in *Baxter v. Montana* (2009). Similar to the American states, Canada (2016), Germany (2015), Finland (2012), and Switzerland (1942) permit physician aid in dying whereby physicians prescribe life-ending medication. The Netherlands (2002), Belgium (2002), and Luxembourg (2009) have similar laws allowing physicians to administer as well as prescribe life-ending drugs, and the Colombian Constitutional Court ruled to permit physicians to administer lethal drugs to hasten death in 1997.[21] Switzerland also permits non-physicians to help terminally ill patients to die so long as their motives are not selfish.

PHYSICIAN ORDERS FOR LIFE-SUSTAINING TREATMENT PARADIGM

Since the 1960s, end of life care planning policies has concentrated on promoting the use of advance directives to protect patients' health care preferences and enhancing patients' access to palliative and hospice care.[22] Both approaches encounter barriers that can preclude patients from retaining control over their end of life treatment. Inaccessible language in advance directives deters some people from completing them. And those who do, often neglect to update them, as their goals and preferences change over time. Heath care professionals and family members are also not always aware that they've been completed or where they are located.

In 1991, a coalition of health care professionals gathered at the Center for Ethics in Health Care at Oregon Health & Science University (OHSU) to determine how they could work together to make advance directives more effective. In 1996, Oregon became the first state to use the POLST form designed for any patients who want to define their treatment preferences, particularly those who have advanced, chronic, progressive illnesses and will face death within twelve months. POLST is designed to document patients' goals for care; it goes further by facilitating conversations among health care professionals to make the patient's plans highly visible and portable from one treatment setting to another (e.g., hospital, nursing home, emergency room) during the final year of life. Although the form's contents and names vary by location (e.g., Physician Orders for Scope of Treatment, or POST, in West Virginia), typically the forms include information regarding the use of cardiopulmonary resuscitation (CPR) and other medical interventions, and treatment directions for multiple situations. POLSTs enhance the legalistic transactional approach to advance care planning by providing patients with a set of portable medical orders that communicate their treatment preferences and aid in bridging the communication gap between patients' goals and preferences and the implementation of care.

As interest in POLST has grown, teams of relevant health care providers and stakeholders formed coalitions that followed Oregon's paradigm. A National POLST Paradigm Task began to assist in program and policy development and to conduct research related to POLST. While the scope of the programs varies across states, today, POLST Paradigm Programs exist in every state and Washington, DC; Brazil, Singapore, Germany, Canada, and Australia also use the paradigm in their end of life decision making.

THE UNITED STATES IN A GLOBAL CONTEXT

When compared to other nations, United States is neither an innovation leader nor laggard. Instead, the slow and fragmented end of life policy adoption patterns mirrors the vast majority of nations without end of life policies. The concept of aid in dying and the laws sanctioning it in the United States are products of subnational policymakers who collectively embrace certain procedural and substantive safeguards. To qualify for a prescription, patients must be at least eighteen years old, have a qualifying terminal illness diagnosis that is expected to result in death soon (requirements range from six months to a year), and the ability to communicate healthcare decisions. Patients must administer the drugs themselves. Except for Montana, which has yet to establish its provisions, patients must make two separate oral requests separated by a minimum of 15 days, which is followed by a written request signed in the presence of two witnesses. Patients must wait at least 48 hours after the oral request before receiving a prescription. Table I.1 provides background information about the aid in dying laws around the world, which can vary significantly from this model.

Table I.1 Physician Prescribed and Administered Aid in Dying States and Countries

Country or State	*Year*	*Physician-Prescribed Aid in Dying (Death with Dignity)*	*Physician-Administered Aid in Dying*	*Method of Legalization*	*Statute or Court Decision*	*Age Requirement*	*Required Diagnosis*	*Waiting Period*
Oregon	1997	Legal	Illegal	Referendum	Oregon Death with Dignity Act, Ballot Measure 16	18	Terminal <6 mo	15 d oral request, 48 h written request
Washington	2008	Legal	Illegal	Referendum	Washington Death with Dignity Act, Ballot Measure I-1000	18	Terminal <6 mo	15 d oral request, 48 h written request
Montana	2009	Legal	Illegal	Court Ruling	*Baxter v. Montana*	None specified	None specified	None specified
Vermont	2013	Legal	Illegal	Legislation	Vermont Patient Choice and Control at the End of Life Act	18	Terminal <6 mo	15 d oral request, 48 h written request
California	2015	Legal	Illegal	Legislation	End of Life Option Act	18	Terminal <6 mo	15 d oral request, 48 h written request
Colorado	2016	Legal	Illegal	Ballot Initiative	End of Life Options Act, Proposition 106	18	Terminal <6 mo	15 d oral request, 48 h written request
DC	2016/17	Legal	Illegal	Legislation	Death with Dignity Act 2015	18	Terminal <6 mo	15 d oral request, 48 h written request

(*Continued*)

Table I.1 (Continued)

Hawaii	2018/19	Legal	Illegal	Legislation	Hawai'i Our Care, Our Choice Act	18	Terminal <6 mo	15 d oral request, 48 h written request
Switzerland	1942	Legal	Illegal	Penal code	Article 114 of the Penal Code of Switzerland	None	None	None
Colombia	1997 2015	Legal	Legal	Court ruling Guidelines published	Article 326 of the 1980 Penal Code	7	Terminal phase	Within 15 d after committee approval
Belgium	2002	Legal	Legal	Legislation	Belgian Act on Euthanasia	None Terminal, children	None, adults 1 mo, nonterminal	None, terminal
Netherlands	2002	Legal	Legal	First legal review procedure	Termination of Life on Request and Assisted Suicide (Review Procedures) Act of 2002	12	None	None
Luxembourg	2009	Legal	Legal	Legislation	Euthanasia and Assisted Suicide Law	18	None	None
Canada	2016	Legal, national Legal, Quebec	Legal, national Legal, Quebec	Legislation, national Legislation, Quebec	C-14	18	None	10 d written request

Data Sources: Ezekiel J. Emanuel, Bregje D. Onwuteaka-Philipsen, John W. Urwin, and Joachim Cohen. Attitudes and Practices of Euthanasia and Physician-Assisted Suicide in the United States, Canada, and Europe. *JAMA* 316, no. 1 (July 2016): 79–90; Death with Dignity. "How Death with Dignity Laws Work," *Death with Dignity*, n.d., https://www.deathwithdignity.org/learn/access/.

Since 1942, Switzerland has allowed physicians to prescribe drugs to hasten death however with far fewer restrictions than the United States. According to Article 115 of the Swiss penal code, physicians can prescribe lethal drugs to anyone who may administer them to anyone, which opens the door for participation by non-physicians as well as requests from patients with non-terminal conditions. The only legal restriction is that participants must not have selfish motives. Since the 1980s, aid in dying organizations such as Exit, Dignitas, Exit International, and Life Circle have offered aid to Swiss residents as well as non-residents. Between 2008 and 2012, 611 people from 31 countries traveled to Switzerland to gain access to lethal drugs.[23] Most of the organizations begin the process with patients drinking sodium pentobarbital, a strong sedative. They then receive a syringe containing a lethal dose of barbiturate and saline mixture. While others can and do assist with administration, the patient must open the needle valve.[24] Over 26,000 members of the nonprofit Exit association pay an annual fee of $40 (equivalent to 40 Swiss Francs) for the assurance that they will receive aid in dying when the time comes.[25] Members must be Swiss residents who are over the age of 20. Dignitas operates on a fee-for-service basis. Since its founding in 1998, the organization has assisted in 2,100 deaths of Swiss and non-Swiss residents. It charges between $4,600 (€4,000) and $8,100 (€7,000) for their services based on whether the organization is taking on any responsibilities for family duties.[26]

The remaining countries in the Table—Colombia, Belgium, the Netherlands, Luxembourg, and Canada—restrict administration to physicians, who can both prescribe and administer life ending medication. Colombia is the only nation in the world that makes aid in dying determinations exclusively on approval of a committee. The scientific committee, comprised of a medical expert, a lawyer, and mental health professional, must agree on whether the patient satisfies the requirements to receive aid in dying.[27] The Netherlands, Belgium, and Colombia are the only counties in the world whose laws permit children to receive aid in dying; the Netherlands permits it at 12, Colombia at 7, and Belgium has had no age restrictions since 2014. Children "in a hopeless medical situation of constant and unbearable suffering that cannot be eased and which will cause death in the short-term" can receive aid in dying with parental approval as well as psychiatric and medical advice.[28] As of this writing, three minors, ages 17, 11, and 9, have received lethal injections in Belgium.[29] Between 2002 and 2015, seven aid in dying cases involving children 12 and older were declared in the Netherlands.[30] There has not been any cases associated with Colombia's Resolution 825 which passed on March 9, 2018.[31]

Only a few countries outside of the United States impose a waiting period. Canadians must wait ten days after submitting a written request. Minors in

Belgium have the most extended waiting period of a month, but Belgian adults have no waiting period at all, and even Dutch children have no waiting period. The laws in Switzerland and Luxembourg also have no provisions for waiting periods.

PUBLIC OPINION AND END OF LIFE POLICIES

On some issues of morality, Americans are increasingly adopting a "live let live" attitude.

According to a Gallup poll, Americans have embraced a liberal outlook on a variety of issues including birth control, divorce, pornography, and aid in dying. In 2001, the year Gallup began measuring the moral acceptability of *doctor-assisted suicide,* 49 percent of respondents personally agreed that aid in dying is morally acceptable. Since 2014, the percentage has remained above 52 percent. The pervasiveness of individual choice in the American medical systems and practices today continues to be integral to the advancement of right to die movement policies. Even if few Americans have them in place for end of life care, today, most support advanced directive laws. A 2009 Pew Research Center report finds that 84 percent of Americans approve of laws that let patients decided whether to be kept alive through medical treatment.[32]

There is an expectation that public opinion influences public policy in democratic nations. Prior to the adoption of the first living will law in the late 1970s, for example, public approval for the laws had been above 70 percent. Even so, most states didn't adopt a law until the mid-1980s when public opinion exceeded 80 percent. Policy adoption was not immediate but lawmakers across states were responsive to the public's preferences. Despite seemingly widespread support, most states remain reluctant to adopt aid in dying legislation.

Responsiveness to public support of aid in dying laws has been noticeably slower than its less controversial than its right to die counterparts. Since the adoption of the first law in Oregon in 1997, only seven jurisdictions in the United States have adopted death with dignity legislation. If a growing number of Americans support aid in dying legislation, why are so few states adopting it?

One explanation could be the semantics problem that shrouds the aid in dying issue. Whether the policy is referred to physician assisted *death* or physician assisted *suicide* directly affects public approval. Voluntary *euthanasia*, which involved physicians ending a patient's life, is illegal in the United States but public support for it is consistently higher than when the question includes the word *suicide.* Support for physician-initiated death has exceeded

50 percent since the 1970s. Seventy-three percent of respondents in 2018 agreed that if a terminally ill patient or his or her family member requests it, doctors should be allowed by law to use painless means to end the patient's life. The aid in dying question, which Gallup began administering in 1996 asks respondents about their attitude about a doctor assisting a patient to commit suicide. Between 1996 and 2013, support for the PAD question averaged 58 percent compared to 69 percent for *euthanasia* question. Since 2014, the averages have increased to 65 percent and 70 percent, respectively, which means Americans are making less of a distinction between the terms. Even so, the fact that a disparity exists may obscure communication to politicians.

There's also the issue of relying on national public opinion data to affect subnational policy change. National public opinion polls, which typically include between 1,000 and 1,500 respondents from all 50 states and the District of Columbia, are representative of a national sample but include too few respondents in each state to be representative of attitudes in each jurisdiction. There are several university studies, think tanks, and smaller polling outlets that are measuring state-level PAD approval, but question wording and frequency varies across surveys. Beyond the continuity problem is the issue of awareness as it is unlikely that state legislators pay attention to studies that may be buried on advocacy/opposition groups websites or in scholarly journal articles. PAD public opinion polls are informative but hardly influential enough to induce policy adoption in the remaining 44 non-adopting states.

THE CHALLENGE OF MORALITY POLICY CHANGE

Whether and how quickly representatives respond to social problems is significantly influenced by policy type and definition. End of life policies are a form of social regulatory policy whereby government imposes or legitimizes values and moral practices. Because most issues are multidimensional, almost every issue is susceptible to framing that connotes "sin," which naturally draws the interest of religious groups. As Kreitzer (2015) points out, religion affects morality policies directly through its adherents by providing a moral code and a collective identity, and indirectly through religious organizations acting as interest groups. Religious organizations, as specialized groups, participate in hundreds of issues. But according to a Pew study, the largest percentage of groups in the study (42 percent) concentrated on life-and-death morality issues, such as abortion, the death penalty, and right to die policies.

When compared to other policy types, morality policies produce systematically different patterns of political behavior which does not always result in legislative responsiveness. Technical simplicity heightens public awareness of and attentiveness to an issue but whether political conflict exists about it is central to legislative responsiveness. Meier refers to morality policies with conflict as two-sided morality issues (e.g., school prayer, gambling, homosexuality) and those where universal opposition exists are labeled as one-sided morality issues (e.g., drunk driving, drug abuse, murder). Extant research suggests that elected officials are more likely to be responsive to public opinion on two-sided morality policies than one-sided morality policies which increases rates of diffusion. Most states, being risk adverse, do not adopt new policies; however, as policy knowledge increases, the rate of adoption increases dramatically and eventually tapers off again as the pool of potential adopters becomes much smaller. Walker finds that the diffusion of policy in a minority of policy areas diffuses across states at a much faster pace. For example, between 1970 and 1974, all but five states adopted no-fault divorce laws.

When morality policies are one-sided, or without partisan competition, however, state policymakers are less inclined to adoption innovation, and when they do, diffusion is slower. For example, abortion and capital punishment are both two-sided morality issues. Within years of the US Supreme Court's landmark decisions *Furman v. Georgia* (1972) and *Roe v. Wade* (1973) the Democratic and Republican Parties added their respective stances on the death penalty and abortion to their platform planks. Since 2016, state legislatures and the District of Columbia have enacted 40 death penalty[33] and 306 abortion-related laws.[34]

The 1970s was also a landmark decade for the right to die issue. The New Jersey Supreme Court decision *In Re Quinlan* (1976) brought national attention to the debate but it would be 36 years before either party "owned" a position in it. In 2012, the National Republican Party added its opposition to non-consensual withholding or withdrawal of care or treatment including food and water and aid in dying to its platform plank on "The Sanctity and Dignity of Human Life."[35] While no entity with political power of any kind had seriously proposed such measures without patient consent since before World War II, the plank staked out ground for Republicans and conservatives indicating they would oppose aid in dying. Until the National Democratic Party takes ownership of the opposing stance, right to die policies will remain one-sided, consensus morality issues that diffuse incrementally.

Issue ownership for the National Democratic Party raises two problems. On the issue of aid in dying, it has been and continues to be a divisive issue along racial, religious and political lines. Minorities are less approving of PAD laws than whites. Only 29 percent of black and 32 percent of Hispanics approve of PAD laws compared to 53 percent of whites. When race is combined with religion, Black Protestants are the least supportive of PAD laws compared to White Mainline Protestants (22 percent and 61 percent, respectively). Still, the largest percentage of PAD supporters are those who are not affiliated with any religious group (66 percent).[36] In terms of political affiliation, higher percentages of support come from those who identify themselves as Democrat or Independent than Republican. Contrary to what national trend data suggests, the landscape of PAD support is mostly comprised of non-religious, white Democrats. Still, America's pervading belief system that values the sanctity of human life, which was also echoed in the US Supreme Court's unanimous decision in *Washington v. Glucksberg* (1997), represents an even bigger problem for the right to die movement. Almost every religion espouses the idea that life is sanctified by divine means external to man, public pronouncements supporting a right to die would be perceived as advocacy for "sin." Since as Meier (1994) points out, no one wants to advocate for sin, a movement continues to persist with growing public approval, few adopting states, and no national political party advocacy.

PLAN OF THE BOOK

The finality of death naturally makes questions of whether and when life should end has always been multidimensional. As Lepore poignantly notes, "Matters of life and death are not, inherently, partisan. They have been turned to partisan purposes, and that shift has fundamentally altered American political culture. Americans have always fought about rights, but life is different from liberty and property."[37] Much has already been written about end of life policies from the medical, legal, and religious perspectives, but less is known about the political aspects of the end of life policymaking process. Despite the various forces that hindered, and in many instances, stymied reform efforts, advocates continue to believe a significant change in public approval will eventually lead to a fundamental right to die. As Hemlock Society's President, Derek Humphry told the *New York Times* in 1991, "It has puzzled me for years why this hasn't taken over from abortion as the major issue because it touches everybody—we're all going to die. Well, it's been a long fight through the wilderness to get a voice, but now we have one—here and now."[38] Nearly 30 years later, he's still only partially correct. Public opinion has improved but widespread legislative responsiveness has not. As Meier's (1994) morality policy framework contends and this book demonstrates, partisanship can't explain the incremental nature of end of life policy diffusion. For most of the right to die movement's history, policy reform efforts have been notably bipartisan. Instead, the ongoing absence of both major political parties in the legislation of the issue continues to have significant impact on the movement's progress over the last century. Because they are one-sided morality policies, or as Meier calls them, the "politics of sin," diffusion will remain incremental.

In fact, advocates' unprecedented ability to overcome conventional beliefs about the sanctity of life in the six death with dignity adopting states and Washington, DC is more of a testiment of how liberal they are comparied to the rest of the country. The book relies on the public policy, interest group, law and society, and health care scholarship to evaluate the various forces that continue to affect states' adoption behavior.

I retrace the legislative history of the right to die movement to shed light various ways end of life policies promulgated without political party prioritization and highlights the subtle demonstrations of partisan politics, which in some states, has already begun to signal a partisan divide. In the beginning, however, there were lone policy advocates, also known as policy entrepreneurs, who had to form new coalitions to affect policy change. The Three Streams Theory provides a theoretical framework in chapters 1 and 2 to evaluate the various forces that stymied progress and to highlight the successful political strategies that led to reform. As the support for physician aid in dying grew, mobilization followed. Chapter 3 builds from the pluralist, transactional/economic, and neo-pluralist perspectives found in the interest group literature to identify the factors that led to the creation of the two foundational aid in dying interest groups—Euthanasia Society of America and the Hemlock Society—and the various internal and external factors that effected their influence on policy reform. Chapter 4 takes a closer look at the complicated relationship between law and society in end of life matters. Specifically, the chapter addresses the three prominent questions the state and federal courts have had to answer regarding a right to die: 1) Is aid in dying a crime?; 2) Where are the lines drawn between terminating or withdraw life-sustaining treatment for competent and incompetent patients?; and 3) Is there a fundamental right for terminally ill patients to initiate death? Chapter 5 discusses the flaws in advance directives that led to POLST, the formation of the National POLST Paradigm Initiative Task Force (NPPTF) as well as the diffusion of innovation of the POLST Paradigm. Finally, chapter 6 summarizes findings and speculates about the future of end of life policies. Mindful of the movement's controversial past, the analysis pays careful attention to the terminology used to describe the act of hastening death by embracing neutral terms such as *physician aid in dying* (PAD), *death with dignity*, and *aid in dying*, as much as is reasonably possible.

NOTES

1. Patient Protection and Affordable Care Act 2010. 2010. *United States Public Laws*. 111th Cong., P. L. 111–48.
2. Patient Self Determination Act of 1990, 42 USC § 1395cc.

3. House Democrats (Tammy Baldwin, D-WI-2, Sand M. Levin, D-MI-12, and Bill Pascrell, D-NJ-8) sponsored the Advance Planning and Compassionate Care Act of 2009 (HR 2911, 111th Cong.), but the Life-Sustaining Treatment and Medical Preferences Act of 2009 (HR 1898, 111th Cong.) and the Advance Planning and Compassionate Care Act of 2009, S 1150, 111th Cong. HR 1898 and S 1150 were bipartisan. The Advance Planning and Compassionate Care Act had also garnered bipartisan support in 2007 (S 464, 110th Cong.), 2002 (S2857, 107th Cong.), 1999 (S 628, 106, Cong.) and 1997 (S 1345, 105 Cong.).

4. Lee Fang, "For 'Death Panels' Before She Was Against Them? Palin Endorsed End of Life Counseling As Governor." *ThinkProgress*, August 13, 2009, https://thinkprogress.org/for-death-panels-before-she-was-against-them-palin-endorsed-end-of-life-counseling-as-governor-95b2ab523aad/.

5. Jim Rutenberg, "Gingrich Faces More Scrutiny over Corporate Clients." *The New York Times*, November 17, 2011, https://www.nytimes.com/2011/11/18/us/politics/newt-gingrich-faces-more-scrutiny-on-corporate-clients.html.

6. Public Law 108–173.

7. Amy Sullivan, "Oh, Those Death Panels." *Time*, August 13, 2009, http://swampland.time.com/2009/08/13/oh-those-death-panels/.

8. Robert Pear, "Obama Returns to End-of-Life Plan That Caused Stir." *New York Times,* December 26, 2010, https://www.nytimes.com/2010/12/26/us/politics/26death.html.

9. Angie Drobnic Holan, "*PolitiFact*'s Lie of the Year: 'Death Panels.'" *PolitiFact,* December 18, 2009, http://www.politifact.com/truth-o-meter/article/2009/dec/18/politifact-lie-year-death-panels/.

10. Sarah Palin, "Statement on the Current Health Care Debate." Facebook, August 7, 2009, https://www.facebook.com/notes/sarah-palin/statement-on-the-current-health-care-debate/113851103434/.

11. Kathy Kiely and Mimi Hall, "End-of-Life Counseling Had Bipartisan Support," *ABC News*, August 17, 2009, http://abcnews.go.com/Politics/story?id=8352602.

12. Pew Research Center for the People and the Press, "Health Care Reform Closely Followed, Much Discussed." *Pew Research Center*, August 20, 2009, http://www.people-press.org/2009/08/20/health-care-reform-closely-followed-much-discussed/.

13. United States Census Bureau, "Older People Projected to Outnumber Children for First Time in US History." *United States Census Bureau*, March 13, 2018, https://www.census.gov/newsroom/press-releases/2018/cb18-41-population-projections.html.

14. Stanford School of Medicine, "Where Do Americans Die," *Stanford School of Medicine,* n.d., https://palliative.stanford.edu/home-hospice-home-care-of-the-dying-patient/where-do-americans-die/.

15. The Economist, "What People Most Want in Their Final Months." *The Economist,* April 29, 2017, https://www.economist.com/international/2017/04/29/what-people-most-want-in-their-final-months.

16. Penelope Wang, "Cutting the High Cost of End of Life Care." *Times*, December 12, 2012, http://time.com/money/2793643/cutting-the-high-cost-of-end-of-life-care/.

17. Emmie Martin, "Most Americans Close to Retirement Have Saved Only 12 percent of What They Need." *CNBC*, May 19, 2018, https://www.cnbc.com/2018/03/19/most-americans-close-to-retirement-have-saved-12-percent-of-what-they-need.html.

18. Christopher Robbins, "Why Many US Households Don't Own Life Insurance." *Financial Advisor*, June 22, 2017, https://www.fa-mag.com/news/why-many-u-s--households-don-t-own-life-insurance-33420.html; Zoe Williams, "Cost of Living? What about the Cost of Being Dead?" *The Guardian*, January 21, 2014, https://www.theguardian.com/commentisfree/2014/jan/21/cost-of-living-what-about-the-cost-of-being-dead.

19. Roz Chast, *Can't We Talk about Something More Pleasant?: A Memoir* (New York: Bloomsbury, 2016).

20. Oregon Ballot Measure 16, Oregon Death with Dignity Act (ORS 127.800-995).

21. Patients Rights Council, "Switzerland." *Patients Rights Council*, n.d., http://www.patientsrightscouncil.org/site/switzerland/.

22. A London physician by the name of Dr. Cicely Sanders introduced hospice care to the United States during a series of lecture in 1963 which led to the formation of the first hospice in Branford, Connecticut in 1973. Hospice care requires a team of health care professionals who work together to offer severely ill or terminally ill patients comfort and pain management as well as emotional and spiritual support. Hospice care is available in an inpatient hospital setting as well as in a home setting for patients nearing death with six months or less to live. Palliative care, which is designed to relieve pain, is offered to all patients; Howard Ball, *The Right to Die: A Reference Handbook*, Contemporary World Issues (Santa Barbara, CA: ABC-CLIO, LLC, 2017); Stephen R. Connor, "Development of Hospice and Palliative Care in the United States." *OMEGA—Journal of Death and Dying* 56, no. 1 (2008).

23. Jacque Wilson, "'Suicide Tourism' to Switzerland has doubled since 2009." *CNN*, August 20, 2014, https://www.cnn.com/2014/08/20/health/suicide-tourism-switzerland/index.html.

24. George Mills, "What You Need to Know About Assisted Suicide in Switzerland." *The Local*, May 3, 2018, https://www.thelocal.ch/20180503/what-you-need-to-know-about-assisted-death-in-switzerland.

25. Samuel Blouin, "'Suicide Tourism' and Understanding the Swiss Model of the Right to Die." *National Post*, May 24, 2018, https://nationalpost.com/pmn/news-pmn/suicide-tourism-and-understanding-the-swiss-model-of-the-right-to-die.

26. George Harrison, "Right to Die? What is Dignitas, Why Do People Go There to End Their Lives and where is the Assisted Dying Clinic in Switzerland?" *The Sun*, May 30, 2018, https://www.thesun.co.uk/news/4245459/dignitas-assisted-dying-clinic-switzerland/.

27. Latin American Post, "Health Ministry Issues Guidelines for Colombian Doctors to Perform Physician-Assisted Suicide." *Latin American Post*, April 27, 2015,

https://www.latinamericanpost.com/index.php/global-issues/10646-health-ministry-issues-guidelines-for-colombian-do.

28. "The Belgian Act on Euthanasia of May 28, 2002." *Ethical Perspectives* 9, nos. 2–3 (2002): 182–88.

29. Charles Lane, "Children are Being Euthanized in Belgium." *The Washington Post*, August 6, 2018, https://www.washingtonpost.com/opinions/children-are-being-euthanized-in-belgium/2018/08/06/9473bac2-9988-11e8-b60b-1c897f17e185_story.html?utm_term=.261fbfd0520f.

30. Alliance Vita, "Euthanasia in the Netherlands." *Alliance Vita*, March 2018, https://www.alliancevita.org/wp-content/uploads/2018/03/euthanasia-in-the-netherlands.pdf.

31. Latin American Post. 2018. "Colombia Has Regulated Euthanasia for Children and Adolescents." *Latin American Post*, March 13, 2018, https://latinamericanpost.com/index.php/human-rights/20090-colombia-has-regulated-euthanasia-for-children-and-adolescents.

32. Pew Research Center, "End-of-Life Decisions: How Americans Cope." *Pew Research Center Social and Demographic Trends*, August 20, 2009, http://www.pewsocialtrends.org/2009/08/20/end-of-life-decisions-how-americans-cope/.

33. National Conference of State Legislatures, "State and Capital Punishment." *National Conference of State Legislatures*, June 6, 2018, http://www.ncsl.org/research/civil-and-criminal-justice/death-penalty.aspx.

34. Guttmacher Institute, "State Policy Trends 2018: With Roe v. Wade in Jeopardy, States Continued to Add New Abortion Restrictions." *Guttmacher Institute*, December 11, 2018, https://www.guttmacher.org/article/2018/12/state-policy-trends-2018-roe-v-wade-jeopardy-states-continued-add-new-abortion.

35. The Democratic Platform did not mention end of life policies.

36. Pew Research Center, "Chapter 1: Opinion about Laws on Doctor-Assisted Suicide." *Pew Research Center*, November 21, 2013, http://www.pewforum.org/2013/11/21/chapter-1-opinion-about-laws-on-doctor-assisted-suicide/.

37. Jill Lepore, *The Mansion of Happiness: A History of Life and Death*. New York: Vintage Books, 2012.

38. Jane Gross, "The 1991 Election: Euthanasia; Voters Turn down Mercy Killing Idea." *New York Times*, November 7, 1991, www.nytimes.com/1991/11/07/us/the-1991-election-euthanasia-voters-turn-down-mercy-killing-idea.html.

Chapter 1

Historical Beginnings

The Policy Entrepreneurs of the Early Aid in Dying Movement

According to Mohandas Gandhi, "Every good movement passes through five stages: indifference, ridicule, abuse, repression, and respect."[1] If reformers endured the first four stages, no matter how mild or severe the trials, success would be inevitable. In the public policy literature, reformers are known as policy entrepreneurs. They may be elected officials, interest group leaders, or ordninary citizens, but they all share a willingness to invest their "time, energy, reputation, and money" to legislate change. They are also as tenatious as they are patient (179). Since policymakers' receptivity to their proposed solutions and willingness to put their issue on the public policy agenda is predicated on the timely confluence of the problem, policy, and politics streams, as Kingdon's Three Streams Theory posits, policy entrepreneurs must wait for "policy windows" to open. Only then will innovation to occur.

The advent of anesthesia in the nineteenth century remedied patients' concerns about pain during surgery but it also gave the medical profession unprecedented and unregulated authority over pain and death issues, blurring the line between relieving pain and accelerating death. Without ethical guidelines, a movement began to emerge that called for government to establish legal boundaries to protect society from potential abuses (the problem stream). The first call for government intervention occurred in 1891 when prominent educator and scholar, Felix Adler, proposed a six-member commission of doctors and judges that would have to unanimously agree to grant aid in dying for the terminally ill. In 1906, policy entrepreneurs' personal and professional experiences with long-suffering and painful deaths led to the movement's initial attempts to legalize physician aid in dying (PAD) (the policy stream). Despite their best efforts, the bills failed (the politics stream). While woman's suffrage, education, child labor, and eugenics Progressive Era movements led to legislative victories, it would take the right die movement 70 years before adoption of the first living will law in California in 1976. Why did it take so long for a "policy window" to open for right to die policy entrepreneurs?

Before the aid in dying movement could achieve its policy goal, it had to address two persisting problems. First, it needed to coalesce around a policy solution. Progressives belief in science, the regularity potential of government, and perfecting human creation equated to "a natural right to natural death" but without the intellectual ability to differentiate eliminating the *defective* (involuntary death) from the promotion of a painless death for the terminally ill (aid in dying). *Eugenics euthanasia*, as it became known, sought to hasten death humanely, albeit by gas poisoning, of society's undesirables (e.g., criminals, the poor, imbeciles). The lingering effect of the Progressive Era's eugenics version of aid in dying created widespread confusion about the motivations for hastening death among the public, policymakers, and even within movement.

They also had to actively build coalitions *outside* of political parties. Since party planks reflect the goals of the party, the exclusion of the issue of a right to die on both party's policy agendas for much of the movement's legislative history meant policy entrepreneurs who sought to enact laws through the legislative process would need to attract the support of partisans but they also understood that neither party, as an organization, would participate in advocacy (or opposition) of their policy.[2] For those who chose to put proposals directly to the voters through the initiative process, building winning coalitions with well-funded and nationally recognized death with dignity organizations took on even greater importance to the success of their campaigns.

Over the next two chapters, the Three Streams Theory provides a framework to examine the policy entrepreneur-led bills and initiatives of the twentieth and twenty-first centuries, to evaluate the various forces that stymied progress, and to highlight the successful political strategies that led to reform. This chapter demonstrates the pervasiveness of the belief that aid in dying reform warranted a public health response which only served to strengthen its ties to the eugenics movement. Only when aid in dying advocates embraced a patient-centered focus did the political tide begin to shift. The next chapter identifies the key actors who were pivotal in changing the course of the aid in dying movement and how policy entrepreneurs have begun to work together to achieve their policy goals.

RIGHT TO DIE LEGISLATION, 1906–1959

Personal appeals have always been a hallmark of end of life policies from the first right to die bills. However, the two earliest bills, dubbed by the media as the "chloroform bills" because of their interest in legislating physician aid in dying through the administration of a lethal dose of chloroform differed from later bills in their singular focus on hastening death and presentation of legalization as a matter of public health.

Anna Hall's crusade led to the Ohio bill. She was an ideal advocate for several reasons. First, she had wealth she had inherited from her parents, which gave her the resources to lobby Congress. Second, she had some degree of fame, also largely inherited; her father, Charles F. Hall, had been an Arctic explorer and she was known to be an active member of the Audubon and Humane societies. At the same time, she was relatable when she drew on her recent experience of losing her mother to cancer, the eighth leading cause of death in the early 1900s.[3] Hall spent years writing letters to notable medical, academic, political, and religious figures, penning newspaper editorials about her views, and giving invited talks on the subject. She eventually drew the attention of Democratic representative Henry T. Hunt, a Yale-educated attorney from Cincinnati, who proposed the bill on January 24, 1906.

"An Act Concerning the Administration of Drugs, etc., to Mortally Injured and Disease Persons," would have enabled the fatally injured, terminally ill, and severely pained and tortured of sound mind to receive an anesthetic from a physician. To ensure that requests were not made under duress, the patient would first have to declare an interest in being put to death in the presence of three witnesses; three "reputable physicians" would have to concur unanimously that the patient's illness was terminal.[4] The bill faced immediate opposition from Representative Elijah Hill from Columbiana County who motioned to have it rejected. Miss Hall watched from the gallery and openly wept as she watched the motion to reject fail, 79 to 19. Even so, many questioned whether the bill provided enough flexibility for patients to change their minds or guidance for physicians to assess their patients' judgment while experiencing debilitating pain. In the latter vein, a letter to the editor of the *New York Times* states:

> The evidence for the people is overwhelming to the effect that in the presence of excruciating pain, soundness of mind is absent. Distinguished members of the medical profession have sworn positively that even a toothache causes mental irritation, that a twinge of the gout may result in a momentary frenzy, that homicidal mania has been caused by a pinch, that manslaughter may follow the puncture of a pin.[5]

The bill died in committee. In response to Hall's proposal, Republican Assemblyman William A. DeGroot of New York proposed legislation that would have specifically criminalized both PAD and advocacy for it. With few supporters, even among aid in dying opponents, the bill was referred to the Committee on Codes where it died. But the stage was set.

Within months of Ohio's bill, a pair of Republican legislators proposed an aid in dying bill in Iowa. Well-respected male politicians, physicians, and eugenics advocates Republican Assemblymen Ross H. Gregory and F. N. Buckingham introduced Iowa House File 367 on March 10, 1906. The Iowa bill was more radical than the Ohio bill, yet it faced considerably less backlash likely due the reputation of its sponsors who legitimized aid in dying in a way that Hall, a female advocate without a medical background, could not at the time. In addition to counteracting a general sense among the public that most doctors opposed PAD, the Iowa bill and its close proximity to the effort in Ohio shed light on two fundamental features about the burgeoning right to die movement. First, the discourse on aid in dying had become a public forum. Once a topic that remained within medical associations and societies, the aid in dying debate now included the press and policymakers in the states. Second, policy advocacy supersedes party affiliation and identity. What the sponsorship of aid in dying bills by legislators on both sides of the isle reveals, and what almost the next century confirms, is a commitment to legalization that transcended party affiliation.

"A Bill for an Act Requiring Physicians to Take Human Life" actually charged physicians with the responsibility to euthanize incurable patients who requested it, making provisions for criminal action against physicians who did not end their patients' suffering by hastening death upon request. The bill stipulated that upon the request of a terminally ill patient request to end his or her life "by artificial means," the treating physician must bring in two other reputable physicians and the county coroner to make the determination and notify the family of their determination. Physicians who refused risked six months to a year's jail time and fines of up to $1,000 (620). Proponents of the bill believed the punitive language in the bill would act as safeguards against potential abuse; others argued that physicians who wished to avoid compliance could simply argue that the patient was not necessarily terminal. The publicity the bill drew from having been read twice without objection and referred to committee was sufficient for its supporters to accept that its passage was unlikely so Buckingham withdrew the measure from consideration. Gregory explained to a reporter that he understood that society was not ready to legalize assisted death, noting that he hoped that his "common sense legislation" would someday "reduce suicides, end the needless pain, and [reflecting the point of view that had led him to champion eugenics] prevent the rearing of idiotic, hopelessly diseased or hideously deformed children" (622).[6]

Public interest in legalizing hastening death was growing. The chloroform bills had solidified the importance of policy entrepreneurs in shaping public discourse. In the 1930s, Inez Celia Philbrick, a physician and faculty member of the University of Nebraska, called upon thirty-two-year-old Nebraska

Senator and attorney John H. Comstock for assistance to draft and introduce the "Voluntary Euthanasia Act" in the state senate.[7] Above and beyond his support for aid in dying, his personal ties to Philbrick, as the physician who had been present at his birth, eagerly drew him to the cause. Philbrick was outside of government, but she had impeccable credentials as a professor and physician who had cared for dying cancer patients. She was also a eugenicist and suffragette. Philbrick's motivation to advocate for assisted death, in part, was a response to the loss of her friend who, despite having spent the last six months of her life bedridden in excruciating pain, declined drugs to hasten death for fear that Philbrick would be criminally sanctioned. Her version of twentieth-century maternal feminism, which was heavily influenced by Darwin's evolutionary theory, grouped birth control, assisted death, and eugenics as women's issues. According to the theory, women's superiority comes from their reproductive capabilities as well their usage of "sexual selection" to determine whose genes would continue to the next generation. Advocacy for aid in dying, as a public health issue, was also the responsibility of women who needed the discretion to remove "living creatures so monstrous, so deficient, so hopelessly insane that their continued existence has for them no satisfactions and entails a heavy burden on society."[8]

Thus, the involvement of eugenicists in introducing of Iowa House File 367 foreshadowed a linkage between assisted death and the eugenics movements that continued beyond the 1930s. The US Supreme Court's decision in *Buck v. Bell* upheld Virginia's state interest in promoting the "health of the patient and the welfare of society" and opened the floodgates for adoption of eugenics sterilization statutes in 32 states by 1937. As a result, it is estimated that between 60,000 and 70,000 men and women deemed "criminals, prostitutes, imbeciles, feeble-minded, and otherwise "defective" were sterilized without consent.

Philbrick's political ally in the state senate, Comstock, introduced Legislative Bill No. 135, "The Voluntary Euthanasia Act" in 1937. The bill was a disappointment to Philbrick, who had sought a comprehensive aid in dying bill that would have made it mandatory for socially undesirables (e.g., idiots, monstrosities, and the criminally insane). The bill mirrors Hall's bill by allowing PAD only for adults of "sound mind" suffering from an "incurable disease." It also included provisions for physicians to involuntarily end the lives of "mental incompetents" and "minors" at the request a next of kin. The process would begin by applying to a district judge, who would then forward the application to a committee of two doctors and a lawyer would give the treating physician permission to end the patient's life.

The bill passed the first reading, was referred after the second reading to the committee on public health and miscellaneous, but ultimately went without vote or approval. As the Three Streams Theory emphasizes, the identification of a problem (problem stream) and availability of a solution (the policy stream) will not ensure policymaker's attentiveness to the problem or receptivity to the solution proposed. While Comstock was instrumental in introducing the bill, Philbrick needed more political allies to support the bill throughout the tenuous legislative process. According to the *Lincoln Journal Star*, Dr. A. L. Miller, the only physician in the legislature, felt the bill had "merit" but also believed that "it is too early for it.[9] It faced opposition from the Nebraska State Medical Association, the University of Nebraska School of Pharmacy, the editor of the *Journal of the American Medical Association* as well as most churches who were increasingly becoming more vocal about their stance on life-and-death morality issues.

Britain created the Voluntary Euthanasia Society in 1935, and social activists and intellectuals in the United States established the Euthanasia Society of America (ESA) in 1938. The organization, comprised of prominent activists in the women's suffrage, birth control, and eugenics movements, promoted the dissemination of information and legalization of the "lawful termination of human life by painless means."[10] With legalization victories in women's suffrage, birth control, and eugenics, and public opinion data collected in the late 1930s finding almost 50 percent of respondents favoring aid in dying legalization, ESA members were confident that advocacy would eventually lead to reform. Nevertheless, collective action could not overcome the ties that existed between hastening death for the terminally ill and mass murdering by Nazi Germany during World War II. Membership dropped with growing awareness of Nazi death programs. The Catholic Church increased its advocacy during the McCarthy Era, describing all forms of assisted death as murder. In the 1970s, aid and dying groups, such as ESA, who changed its name to Society for the Right to Die (SRD), took on names that communicated a patient-centric message that would allow them to completely distance themselves from the term "euthanasia" and its ties to eugenics.

THE EXPANSION OF THE AID IN DYING POLICIES, 1960–1974

To distance themselves from the collective welfare, social Darwinian themes prevalent in the eugenics discourse after the 1960s, modern aid in dying advocates concentrated on establishing an individual's right to die. Policies that sanctioned aid in dying remained a goal, but policy entrepreneurs also began to use a spectrum of approaches designed to ensure the proper execution and legal protection of patients' choice to hasten death. The first proposal reflecting the movement's new direction would come from a sixty-year-old family doctor and surgeon turned congressman, Walter W. Sackett (D-FL). Because of his failure to build coalitions inside and outside of the statehouse, Glick describes Sackett as "a powerless, freshmen back-bencher." He had lost his son in an automobile accident in 1960, which sensitized him to the plight of parents who were legally obligated to keep their brain-dead children alive. Sackett is credited as the first to propose a constitutional amendment for the "right to die with dignity."[11] In 1967, his 82-word proposed amendment elicited an hour-long debate in the House but was ultimately voted down. He tried proposing the same bill in 1969 but withdrew it because of lack of support.[12]

The bipartisan members of the Health and Welfare Committee of the Idaho House of Representative were more optimistic. Their "Voluntary Euthanasia Act of 1969" would have permitted PAD following certification of patients' incurable and terminal illnesses by two physicians, a signed declaration in the presence of two witnesses, and a waiting period of a month. Under the law, anyone caught "willfully concealing, destroying or falsifying" a patient's declaration would be guilty of first-degree murder. The declaration would remain in place for the remainder of patients' lives unless they countermanded it, however.[13] While the inclusion of a waiting period and chances for patients to change their minds had been designed to address resistance, the bill failed in committee.

Over the next several years, Representative Sackett channeled his mission to establish a right to die into the first proposed living will law. Fla. HB 3184 enabled patients to document their interest life-sustaining treatment during the final days of a terminal illness. For the mentally competent, the bill is straightforward—patients would need to have the document recorded with the clerk of the circuit court. However, the steps involved for those who are incapable of making decisions on their own (e.g., the mentally disabled and minors) and his primary focus—wards in mental health facilities—presented opportunities for abuse by patients' families or physicians who could deem prolonging life pointless. Specifically, a close member of the family (e.g., spouse, immediate kin) or three physicians (when no kin is available), along with the approval of a circuit judge, would decide for the patient. One of the more controversial, and he believed, most urgent provisions in the bill would have allowed indigent people with mental illness and without family, or as he referred to them "the states' mongoloids," to die if they contracted any illness, including infections normally treatable with antibiotics that could lead to death, which he justified as a cost-savings measure to avoid statewide "economic bankruptcy." In fact, he projected a savings of $5 million over the next half century if the state allowed them to "succumb to pneumonia."[14]

The active involuntary death portions of the bill not only sealed its fate (in 1971 and again in 1972);[15] it also doomed any chance of garnering public or interest group support. The Florida Association of Retarded Citizens, the

Florida Medical Association, and Florida Catholic Conference (FCC) actively lobbied against it. Sackett received his most promising response to living will legislation in 1973 Fla. HB 407, which permitted living wills for competent adults but did not declare a right to to die, passed the House Judiciary Committee and a Senate Committee. Unfortunately, the bill died on the calendar a week before the end of the legislative session. Never in the United States had the right to die movement achieved legislative success in both chambers. Still, it would take years before the political environment would be receptive to adopting the country's first living will law.

Between 1971 and 1974, five states—Wisconsin, Washington, Massachusetts, Delaware, and Maryland—introduced living will bills. In 1971, the Wisconsin State Senate introduced a "Right to Die with Dignity" Bill by request, which would have enabled patients to document their desire to end life-sustaining treatment but failed to enumerate safeguards. After two readings and public hearings, the bill died in the Judiciary Committee. The Governor of Washington's Task Force on Aging requested three members of Senate of the State of Washington to introduce a "Death with Dignity" Bill in 1973. The Senate Committee on Social and Health Services opposed the bill and it died in committee. Strong opposition also led to the demise of the living will bills introduced in Massachusetts and Delaware in 1973 and Maryland in 1974.

Oregon Republican Governor Tom McCall's public support of right to die activists led to a group of senators to introduce two bills in 1973. The first was a strong assisted death bill that stipulated that the Department of Human Resources regulate the certification and verification processes in the state. When this failed, another advocated for death with dignity. The bills faced opposition from the public as well as from the Roman Catholic bishops leading to revisions that caused them to die eventually in committee.

In Montana the impetus for legislative action on the right to die started with a woman from Alberton by the name of Joyce Franks whose eighty-six-year-old father's hip fracture led to a lingering death. He sought a lethal dose of medication to end his life from his doctor but was denied. When the Delegates to the 1972 convention asked residents to submit policy ideas for the new constitution, Franks submitted the proposal, "Every citizen be allowed to choose the manner in which he dies." In 1972 she spoke before the Bill of Rights Committee of the Montana Constitutional Convention for the addition of a right to die in the revised Declaration of Rights. Her testimony drew national attention but her proposal was not recommended by the committee for the constitution. After mounting a grassroots effort that involved writing letters to legislators, physicians, and ministers, Democratic representative William C. Hodges introduced of an assisted death bill in the Montana House in 1973.[16] The measure was voted down by the Committee on Public Health, Welfare, and Safety, 76 to 15. The same bill was reintroduced with the title

"Montana Self-Determination of Death Act" of 1975 but the same committee voted it down, 84 to 10.[17]

The consistent defeat of legislative measures aside, the issue of aid in dying had become more salient in the courts, among the public and policymakers, but continued to remain out of the purview of the national Democratic and Republican Parties platforms. The number of *mercy killing* cases increased from eight between 1969 and 1979 to nearly thirty between 1980 and 1985 (135). The Quinlan case and the adoption of living will laws in 1970s also contributed to growing public approval of aid in dying. According to Gallup public opinion data, support for legalization nearly doubled from 37 percent in 1947 to 60 percent in 1977. Surprisingly, however, as the national parties added other divisive issues to their national—abortion and capital punishment—in the 1970s, the parties remained reluctant to take a stance on a right to die.[18]

CONCLUSION

Well before the formation and mobilization of aid in dying interest groups and even in the decades after, activists, fueled by their personal experiences with painful death, occupied the legislative frontlines of the right to movement. Without major parties framing the issue and shaping the debate, reform efforts would depend exclusively on policy entrepreneurs, who, for many decades, and in varying degrees, struggled with separating the eugenics movement from their own. To their credit, their attempts put aid in dying on states' agendas but failed to render policy reform. Collective efforts to denounce eugenics and formulating its goals as movement was a start, but for innovation to occur, the movement would need a "policy window" to open. The three streams finally converged in 1976 when a legal battle involving the fate of a young woman in a persistant vegatative state by the name of Karen Quinlin put the right to die debate on the national agenda.

NOTES

1. Mohandas Gandhi, *Young India,* 1921.

2. The Republican Party's 2012 Platform Plank on "The Sanctity and Dignity of Human Life," strongly opposes aid in dying. The Democratic Platform makes no mention of either or other end of life related policies.

3. Centers for Disease Control, "Leading Causes of Death, 1900–1998," *Centers for Disease Control*, n.d., https://www.cdc.gov/nchs/data/dvs/lead1900_98.pdf (accessed March 7, 2018).

4. Ohio HB 145, 1906.

5. Augustus Tomlinson, "A Case of Euthanasia. In Cultured Tierra del Fuego an Unjust Decision Was Rendered," *New York Times,* February 2, 1906.

6. "Bill to Kill Incurables," *Chicago Tribune*, March 1906, p. 6, col. 1.

7. Legislative Act 105.

8. Inez C. Philbrick, "Further Reflections on Euthanasia," n.d., ICP, Ms 1058, Scrapbook.

9. *Lincoln Journal Star,* February 3, 1937, p. 6.

10. *Euthanasia Society of America*, "Certificate of Incorporation," November 28, 1938.

11. Fla. HJR 91, § 1 (1969) proposed Fla. Const. art. I, § 2).

12. In 1969, Democratic Representative Richard Hodes and along with Sackett introduced House Joint Resolutions 2575 that emphasizes how investing in prolonging all lives reduces opportunities for life-saving techniques for those who could benefit from them. HJR 2575 (1976) at 1.

13. Idaho HB 143, 1969.

14. "Five Year Campaign in Miami: 'Death with Dignity' Gaining. *San Francisco Examiner,* January 26, 1973.

15. He proposed the same bill in 1971 (Fla. HB 68 [1971]) and 1972 (Fla. HB 2614 [1972]). In 1972, He proposed House Resolution 2830 that called on then-Democratic Governor Reubin O. Ashew to commission to study and recommendations related to the process of death. History of Legislation, 1972. Regular Session, History of House Bills at 180, HR 2830.

16. House Bill 137, "An Act to Provide for Voluntary Euthanasia for Certain Individuals with Terminal Illnesses Subject to the Attending Physicians Determination that the Individual Has Voluntarily Requested Euthanasia; and Providing Penalties for Violation of the Act."

17. House Bill 256, "An Act to Allow Montana Citizens to Choose for Themselves How They Shall Die When Their Times Come to Die; Providing for a Legal, Quick, and Painless Death for Those Who Qualify and Request It; and Providing Penalties for Violation of the Act" was introduced by Democratic state representative Bob Finley.

18. Ted Mellnik, Chris Alcantara, and Kevin Uhrmacher, "What Republicans and Democrats Have Disagreed On, from 1856 to Today." *Washington Post*, July 15, 2016, https://www.washingtonpost.com/graphics/politics/2016-election/conventions/party-platform-evolution/.

Chapter 2

Modern Renewal

State End of Life Policy Adoptions

The frequency of right to die bills appearing on states' agendas by the mid-1970s signaled a growing interest in legislative reform. A Gallup poll conducted in California in 1975 indicated significant support for passive (87 percent) and active (63 percent) right to die laws. As living will legislation grew in popularity, a New Jersey Supreme Court case ignited a national discourse on the right to refuse treatment. In April 1975, twenty-one-year-old Karen Quinlan, who was in a coma but not brain dead, was placed on a respirator but had no hope of recovery. Despite her parent's instance to remove the respirator so she could die, the hospital refused, arguing that removal would be homicide. The New Jersey Supreme Court based its decision to order the removal of the respirator on the fact that she was not brain dead, the court's expansive interpretation of the constitutional right to privacy, as well as the right of parents to act as guardians.[1] It is unlikely living will legislation would have changed *Quinlan*. Given her young age, she probably would not have had a living will and even if she did, most laws at the time would not have treated her condition as terminal which would have legally prohibited its execution. Nevertheless, within months of the *Quinlan* decision, California passed the Natural Death Act, the nation's first living will law in 1976.[2]

For much of the 1980s, the right to die policy entrepreneurs focused exclusively on protecting of patient's rights to withdraw or refuse treatment. However, international decriminalization of physican aid in dying laws (PAD) aroused new interest among some activists to return to the movement's policy roots by lobbying for a patient's right to initate death. Over the last several decades, voters and lawmakers alike have increasingly embraced the idea of allowing patients to have the option to choose painless means to end their lives. During the 2017/2018 legislative session alone, 21 state legislatures considered death with dignity statutes. Still, only seven jurisdictions in the

United States have adopted PAD laws. If public opinion cannot explain states' adoption behavior, what does? To answer the question, the chapter continues its exploration of the policy entrepreneurs who navigated the problem, political, and policy environments to affect change. With a focus on the legislative wins of the modern right to die movement, the chapter is specifically interested in identifying common themes among adopting and utilizing states. Evidence suggests that even as the National Democratic Party remains silent on PAD, reform tends to occur in Democratic-led states where religious organizations have less of an impact on voters. Utilization of the laws, however largely remains limited to older, married, educated, whites.

THE INTRODUCTION OF LIVING WILL LAWS

California's law had been introduced by then Democratic Assemblyman Barry Keene. Policy entrepreneurs have historically been fueled by personal and professional encounters with the terminally ill but lacked political or group support (or both) to achieve policy goals. Keene was different. He successfully united the problem, political, and policy streams that Kingdon describes. He was an attorney whose personal experience began when, his neighbor sought his counsel to determine how his terminally ill wife could legally refuse life-sustaining treatment for cancer. His discovery that she had no such right got him interested in the subject; when his mother-in-law faced the same issue in 1972, the newly elected assembly member sought to pass a law that would protect terminally ill patients' medical treatment decisions.[3]

Effective policy advocacy and lobbying directs attention to a policy issue and gets the issue on the legislative agenda, but neither act secures policy adoption. As Glick explains, an inside and outside political strategy is needed to cultivate a winning coalition. Keene had begun his political career with the political savvy to secure leadership support, although the first hearing of his living will legislation, in 1974, failed. He had won a guarantee of a hearing on the living will legislation, as well as placement on the Committee on Health, by supporting Leo T. McCarthy's bid for speaker of the assembly. In 1974, he hastily proposed a bill that stated that "every person has the right to die without prolongation of life by medical means." As Glick (94) argues, overreliance on "insider status" coupled with strong opposition from the California Pro-Life Council (CPLC) and the California Catholic Conference (CCC) confirmed the bill's defeat.[4]

Recognizing the need for outside support and media attention, before reintroducing the bill in 1976, Keene negotiated with powerful outside groups and drew media attention to the issue. Of the more powerful and well-organized opposition groups, the CPLC, the CCC, and the California Medical

Association (CMA), he focused on the latter two. CMA was a ready ally; it recognized the need for a living will law that would protect the liability of doctors who faced drastic increases in medical malpractice insurance costs. The CCC was also sufficiently open to being a potential source of support, which the CPLC was not; the CCC was to the left of many Catholic advocacy groups in other parts of the country. News releases and ongoing media coverage on the right die debate contributed to its salience. The "National Death Act," which had been amended nine times, passed the California legislature by a substantial majority and Governor Jerry Brown signed it. It's enactment on January 1, 1977 represented the beginning of patients having personal control over their own lives. It did not take long however for CMA and California physicians to realize that living wills would not solve the medical malpractice insurance crisis or assuage physician's fears of liability. A 14-day waiting period following a terminal illness diagnosis made them ineffective for half or more patients who lapsed into comas before the terminal diagnosis.

Nevertheless, California's innovation quickly spread nationwide. In 1977, seven proposals for right to die legislation were introduced in state legislatures. In 1979 there were 40. By 1987, 39 states had living will laws. A legal transactional approach to advance care planning that relied on detailed standardized formalities to protect against abuse and error had been established. It would give way to Physician Orders for Life-Sustaining Treatment (POLST) in the 1990s.

THE REBIRTH OF HASTENING DEATH POLICIES

The momentum that grew in the 1980s reflected in part the decriminalization of PAD in the Netherlands, which ignited an international movement. Hemlock Society's Oregon Right to Die and Oregon Death with Dignity Legal Defense and Education Center (ODLDEC) collaborative efforts resulted in the passage of the United States' first physician aid in dying law, "Oregon's Death with Dignity Act" (ODWDA), by referendum in 1997.[5] An ongoing battle for the legalization of death with dignity across the country ensued.

Eager to replicate Oregon's victory in other states and armed with public opinion data demonstrating overwhelming support (between 68 and 74 percent) favoring death with dignity legislation between 2004 and 2017, 200 ODWDA-modeled legislative proposals and three initiative campaigns were introduced in 36 states and the District of Columbia.[6] Over the last twenty-two years, however, six additional death with dignity statutes have passed, in Washington (2008), Vermont (2013), California (2015), Colorado (2016), the District of Columbia (2016/2017), and Hawaii (2018/2019). All but one—Vermont—were efforts led by policy entrepreneurs. As Kingdon's Three Streams Theory posits, the convergence of the problem, policy, and politics streams remain critical to innovation adoption. After decades of attempts, growing coalitions in the California and Hawaii legislatures facilitated the speedy adoption of death with dignity. In Washington, Colorado, and the District of Columbia, however, the reputation of the policy entrepreneurs and the strategies employed contributed significantly to the measure's success. Still, what uniquely distinguishes early aid in dying policy entrepreneurs from today's death with dignity pioneers is their ability to draw interest group support, particularly that of the national death with dignity interest group leaders—Death with Dignity National Center and Compassionate Choices.

Two major players in the campaign for the Washington Death with Dignity Initiative of 2008 (Ballot Measure I-1000-2008) exemplify the importance of connections. Eli Stutsman, the Oregon attorney and lead drafter of the Oregon Death with Dignity Act, had written the legislation, and Washington State's former Democratic Governor Booth Gardner was its sponsor. Suffering from Parkinson's disease, Gardner had become committed to "lessening the pain of dying."[7] He garnered support for the initiative campaign from a host of right to die interest groups including the Death with Dignity National Center.[8] Voters had rejected a similar ballot initiative in 1991 in spite of public opinion data indicating that two out of three Washington voters favored physician aid in dying.[9] Like its predecessor, I-1000 was a collaborative effort among national right to die organizations. However, this time, the law took a more conservative approach by exclusively concentrating on physicians' aid in dying instead of Initiative 119's effort to legalize physician-*assisted* and physician-*performed* death to mentally competent, terminally ill adult patients.

The death with dignity movement reached another significant milestone with Washington State's measure—for the first time in its history, proponents contributed more money than its opposition, which included the Coalition Against Assisted Suicide, led by the Roman Catholic Church, religious groups, the state's medical association, hospice and palliative care works, and nurses.[10] The relatively small number of people in Oregon dying by lethal injection since its law's passage in 1997 challenged opponents' claims that the law would have the most significant adverse effect on the disabled and financially vulnerable.[11] The initiative won by a margin of 58 percent to 42 percent. The law (RCW 70.245) took effect March 5, 2009.

California would join Washington and Oregon. Brittany Maynard's death in 2014 was the catalyst. At twenty-nine years old, with an inoperable brain cancer diagnosis, Maynard left California to access Oregon's Death with Dignity law. State lawmakers in more than a dozen states as well as the District of

Columbia introduced right to die legislation in response, but only California's was rapidly successful.

Notwithstanding its status as the birthplace of the Hemlock Society and the site of the first living will law, California had failed to pass a right to die ballot initative in 1986 and another in 1992. Had Proposition 161, the "California Death with Dignity Act," passed in 1992, physicians would have been able to prescribe lethal drugs to patients and participate in the "painless human and dignified" death of qualifying patients.

Democratic lawmakers made seven attempts to pass aid in dying bills between 1992 and 2012 but again faced opposition from a consortium of health professionals and disability rights activists led by the CCC as well as the CMA.[12] Hopeful that the international attention Maynard's story drew to the death with dignity movement would finally open a policy window in her home state, less than two months after her death, state senators Bill Monning (D-Carmel) and Lois Wold (D-Davis) introduced SB 128, "End of Life Option Act," on January 21, 2015. It received committee and full senate approval, but the Roman Catholic Church's efforts to persuade the state assembly's Heath Committee to vote against the measure effectively ensured that the measure would not pass the assembly, so its sponsors pulled the bill. Democratic governor Jerry Brown called a special session to address the state's healthcare funding problems, which inspired a new set of legislators, Susan Talamantes Eggman (D-Stockton), a former hospice work and the bill author, and Mark Stone (D-Monterey Bay) who reintroduced the bill as ABX2-15, the "End of Life Option Act," in the state assembly. It passed both chambers in September 2015. Brown, a devout Roman Catholic, former Jesuit seminarian, and cancer survivor, confessed himself morally conflicted about the bill but signed it in October 2015.[13] With that California became the fourth state to adopt an aid in dying law, the "End of Life Option Act" of 2015.[14] In his letter to the California Assembly, Brown explained that "The crux of the matter is whether the State of California should continue to make it a crime for a dying person to end his life, no matter how great his pain and suffering."[15]

Colorado followed suit in 2016. It had been one of ten states to propose PAD legislation in 1995, after Oregon's Death with Dignity Act.[16] Declaring that death with dignity "would be the law of the land in a decade," then-freshman Democratic Representative Peggy Lamm proposed Colorado's first two Death with Dignity bills—House Bill 95-1308, "Enactment of Referred Measure on Colorado Dignity in Death Act" in 1995, and House Bill 96-1185 "Colorado Dignity in Death Act" in 1996. Both were defeated in committee.

The 2014 death of Brittany Maynard led Democratic Representatives Lois Court, Joann Ginal, and Lucía Guzmán to introduce House Bill 15-1135 "Terminally Ill Individuals End of Life Decisions" in January 2015. According

Democratic Representative Dianne Primavera committee chair of the House Committee on Public Health Care and Human Services, "The Dems that I've talked to, a lot of them are also split. It's not like we're voting on raising a fee on some sort of driver's license or something. I mean, this is life or death."[17] She along with another Democrat joined Republicans in killing the bill.[18]

In 2016, in response to concerns about a lack of safeguards to ensure families would not hasten the death of terminally ill patients to collect life insurance, State Representatives Court and Ginal introduced HB 16-1054 "Concerning End of Life Options for Individuals with Terminal Illness" while Democratic State Senator Michael Merrifield sponsored a companion bill, SB 16-025, the "Colorado End of Life Options Act." The bill passed the House Judiciary Committee, but the Senate State, Veterans, and Military Committee killed it, and sponsors pulled the bill before it reached the House floor, knowing it would not get enough votes to pass.[19]

Frustrated by the legislature's failures yet driven by the overwhelming public support for aid in dying, attorney Julie Selsberg and civil liberties activist Jaren Ducker petitioned for the Colorado "End of Life Options Act," known as Proposition 106, to be put before the voters as a ballot initiative. Before her father, Charles Selsberg's, slow and painful death from amyotrophic lateral sclerosis, or Lou Gehrig's disease, Selsberg helped him compose a letter to the *Denver Post*, titled "Please, I want to die" begging legislators to "show mercy on the terminally ill. Please."[20] Following his March 2014 death, Selsberg continued the fight. Mirroring Oregon's law and backed by national and state interest groups including the Compassion & Choices Action Network and Compassion and Choices, voters approved Proposition 106 by an unprecedented 2 to 1 margin (65 percent to 35 percent) making Colorado the fifth jurisdiction to adopt an aid in dying law.[21]

The District of Columbia was next, in 2016. The District's progressive stance on other controversial social issues including same-sex marriage and marijuana liberalization hinted at its receptivity to death with dignity. In January 2015, tenured George Washington University law professor and Democratic Councilmember Mary M. Cheh (D-Ward Three) introduced the first death with dignity bill in Washington, DC, the "Death with Dignity Act of 2015," which contains the same stringent safeguards as Oregon's death with dignity legislation, allows terminally ill patients with less than six months to live to obtain lethal drugs from their physicians for self-administration *after* mental competency and diagnosis verifications, waiting periods, and a discussion with a health professional about other options. Public opinion also seemed to favor legalization. A poll conducted by Lake Research July 2015 revealed that 67 percent of Washingtonians favored the measure.[22] The bill also drew the support of the Gay and Lesbian Activist Alliance of Washington, DC, who for the first time, made death with dignity an issue of priority.[23]

With only Yvette Alexander (Ward 7) and Brianne Nadeau (Ward 1) voting no, the bill passed the full Council with a vote of 11 to 2 twice in November. Mayor Muriel Bower's signage in December 2016 made DC the sixth jurisdiction in the nation to adopt an aid in dying statute.[24]

Almost immediately, Congress exercised its authority to veto legislation adoption by the federal district by introducing companion resolutions voicing its disapproval of the law. Senator James Lankford (Oklahoma-R) and Representative Brad Wenstrup (R-Ohio-R) introduced resolutions less than a week receiving the Act for review, but they failed to reach the House floor or Senate by the February 17 deadline.[25] The Act took effect on February 18, 2018, and implementation began on June 6, 2017. The following month, with a vote of 28 to 24, Representative Andy Harris (R-MD) introduced an amendment that would repeal the Act and prohibit the District from spending any funds on its implementation. Cheh called on Congress not to prolong the suffering of District residents who could not afford to relocate to Oregon, Washington, Vermont, California, or Colorado.[26] "This is about the people of the District of Columbia, and whether they can have any control over their own lives," she reminded them.[27] The appropriations bill to repeal the law passed in the House but was not taken up by the Senate Committee on appropriations and was excluded from the final FY 18 omnibus appropriations bill signed into law March 2018 thus protecting the law.[28]

Advocates for Hawaii succeeded in 2018 after near-constant attempts for almost two decades.[29] In 2002, after witnessing his mother's suffering before her death, Democratic Governor Benjamin J. Cayetano proposed Hawaii House Bill 2487, which could have made Hawaii the second state to guarantee a right to die. Despite having enlisted Eli Stutsman, the author of Oregon's law, considerable support from local and national organizations including the American Civil Liberties Union of Hawai'i and a 72 percent approval voter approval rating, the measure failed. The Roman Catholic Church led the opposition, convincing three Catholic Democrats to switch their position the night before the vote, so the bill failed by two votes, 14 to 11.[30]

In their unwavering commitment to adopt PAD in Hawaii, between 2017 and 2018 legislative sessions, Democrats in the House and Senate introduced nine different PAD bills.[31] The last, HB 2739, known as Hawai'i Our Care, Our Choice Act, was introduced by House Majority Leader Representative Della Au Belatti (D-Makiki) on January 24, 2018. The bill moved speedily through the House and Senate committees and in less than a month, the full House voted 39 to 12 and the full Senate 23 to 2 in favor of the bill. On April 5, 2018, surrounded by lawmakers and supporters, Governor David Ige signed the bill into law, making Hawaii the seventh jurisdiction in the nation to give terminally ill patients the choice to receive medication to end their lives. For the first time making a connection between the movement and one of the political parties, Governor Ige told the press that "Every other living democratic governor [should] also support this merciful action to make dying less terrifying and far more peaceful for those up against a tortured passing."[32] The "Our Care Our Choice Act" (Act 002, HB 2739) took effect January 1, 2019.

COMMON FEATURES AMONG ADOPTING STATES

To determine the extent to which partisan politics exists in PAD policymaking, tables 2.1 and 2.2 provide a summary of political aspects of each law including the names and party affiliation of the sponsors and supporters, the names of supporting interest groups, and the vote breakdown. Undeniably, PAD is a partisan issue. Not one Republican sponsored a PAD policy in any of the seven states. Of the four states that adopted their law via state legislature or council, Vermont is the only one wherein Republicans voted in favor of their state's PAD legislation.

Beyond a strong Democratic presence in the states, adopting states also have fewer religious adherents which lessens the influence of opposing religious organizations. In the spectrum of beliefs permeating American politics, the Roman Catholic and evangelical Protestant churches are the most prolific. Of the 70.6 percent of the US population that are Christian, most people identify as either evangelical Protestants (25.4 percent), or Catholic (20.8 percent).[33] It follows that they are also the most prominent of national religious advocacy organizations. While attitudes about life-and-death morality issues varies within the Protestant denomination,[34] the Catechism of the Catholic Church is explicit in opposing PAD or "putting an end to the lives of handicapped, sick, or dying persons" (2277). As the previous section explains and table 2.1 demonstrates, Catholic Church affiliated organizations were strong opponents of PAD in the adopting states but were unsuccessful in rallying public support. According to Gallup data, residents of Pacific and New England states tend to be the least religious. In fact, only eight of the 48 continental states have less than 80 percent of their residents identifying as Christian, half of which are PAD adopting states—Washington (79 percent), Colorado (78 percent), California (76 percent), and Oregon (76 percent).[35]

Interestingly, as diverse as the party that sponsors and votes for PAD, utilization continues to be homogenous. Table 2.3 presents demographics of decedents in Oregon, Washington, and the Netherlands, and Belgium (the only jurisdictions for which data are available). Consistently, PAD opponents in the United States have argued that legalization will exert pressure on the poor, minorities, the disabled, and other marginalized groups. However, the data shows that aid in dying decedents are typically white, between the ages of 65 and 84, married

Table 2.1 Legislative History of Death with Dignity Laws Adopted by Legislatures or Councils

State	Name	Date of Passage	Number of Legislative Sponsors	Sponsors & Political Supports	Vote Breakdown By Party				
					Vote	Democrat	Republican	Independent	Total
California	End of Life Option Act (ABX2-15 (AB-15)	October 16, 2015	33	Luis Alejo (D), Rob Bonta (D), Susan Eggman (D), Bill Monning (D), Mark Stone (D), Lois Wolk (D), Ben Allen (D), Toni Atkins (D), Marty Block (D), Autumn Burke (D), David Chiu (D), Kansen Chu (D), Jim Cooper (D), Kevin de Leon (D), Jim Frazier Jr. (D), Cristina Garcia (D), Steve Glazer (D), Isadore Hall III (D), Loni Hancock (D), Ed Hernandez (D), Bob Hertzberg (D), Jerry Hill (D), Hannah-Beth Jackson (D), Reggie Jones-Sawyer Sr. (D), Mark Leno (D), Evan Low (D), Kevin McCarty (D), Mike McGuire (D), Holly Mitchell (D), Henry Perea (D), Bill Quirk (D), Anthony Rendon (D), Bob Wieckowski (D)	Yea	23	0	0	58%
					Nay	1	14	0	38%
					Abstained	2	0	0	5%

(Continued)

Table 2.1 (Continued)

State	Name	Date of Passage	Number of Legislative Sponsors	Sponsors & Political Supports	Vote Breakdown By Party				
					Vote	Democrat	Republican	Independent	Total
DC	Death with Dignity Act (B21-0038)	Dec. 19, 2016		Cheh (D)	Yea Nay	10 2		1	84.61% 15.39%
Hawai'i	Our Care, Our Choice Act (HB 2739)	April 5, 2018	9	au Belatti (D), Hashem (D), Lowen (D), Luke (D), Morikawa (D), Nishimoto (D), Saiki (D), Takayama (D), Todd (D)	Aye(s) Noes	23 2			76.47% 23.53%
Vermont	Patient Choice and Control at the End of Life Act (Act 39)	May 20, 2013	5	Senate Committee on Health and Welfare (All Democrats)	Yeas Nays	18 6	4 1	 1	73.33% 26.66%

Table created by author from each bill's legislative history.

Table 2.2 Legislative History of Death with Dignity Laws Adopted by Ballot Initiative or Referendum

State	*Name*	*Date of Passage*	*Sponsors & Political Supporters*	*Supporting Organizations & Individuals*	*Opposition Organizations & Individuals*
Colorado	End of Life Options Act (Prop. 106)	November 8, 2016	Gov. John Hickenlooper (D), Sen. Lucia Guzman (D), Sen. Michael Merrifield (D), Reb. Lois Court (D), Rep. Joann Ginal (D), Former Attorney General J.D. MacFarlane (D), Former State Treasurer Cary Kennedy (D), Former Sen. Greg Brophy (R), Former Sen. Donna Johnson (D), Former Sen. Bob Bacon (D)	ACLU Of Colorado, Art of Land, Axiom Action, Boulder Medical Society, The Colorado Community Network, Denver Medical Society, JohnstonWells Public Relations, Libertarian Party of Colorado, MIND Science Spiritual Center, NARAL Pro-Choice Colorado, New Era Colorado, Peoples Legal Alternative Network, ProgressNow Colorado, Pueblo County Medical Association, Pueblo Medical Society, Putnam Transportation Solutions, Selig & Associates, The Safe Center, Dan Diaz, husband of Brittany Maynard	Gov. John "Pete" Ricketts ® of Nebraska, Sen. Larry Crowder (R-35), Former U.S. Rep. Bob Beauprez (R-7), Not Dead Yet Colorado, Coloradans Against Asisted Suicide, Focus on the Family, Colorado Christian University, The Church of Jesus Christ of Latter-Day Saints Office of the First Presidency, John Stonestreet, President of the Chuck Colston Center for Christian Worldview, Colorado Catholic Conference, Archdiocese of Denver, Roman Catholic Diocese of Colorado Springs, Archdiocese of Kansas City in Kansas
Oregon	Oregon Death with Dignity Act (Measure 51)	November 4, 1997	Barbara Coombs Lee, RN, JD, Cheryl K. Smith, JD.	Oregon Right to Die PAC, Oregon Death with Dignity Legal Defense and Education Center,	Oregon Catholic Conference, Ecumenical Ministries of Oregon, National Right to Life Committee, Oregon Medical Association

(Continued)

Table 2.2 (Continued)

State	*Name*	*Date of Passage*	*Sponsors & Political Supporters*	*Supporting Organizations & Individuals*	*Opposition Organizations & Individuals*
Washington	Washington Death with Dignity Act (Initative 1000)	Nov. 4, 2008	Governor Booth Gardner (D), Governor Daniel J. Evans (R), Tom Preston, Dorothy H. Mann, PhD, MPH, Rev. Bruce Parker, D. Min, Kinda N. Olson, PhD, RN.	Oregon Death with Dignity, Compassion & Choices of Washington, Andrew Ross, Loren Parks, Judy Sebba, Compassion and Choices Action Network, Stephen G. Clapp.	Coalition Against Assisted Suicide, Margarita Prentice, State Senator and nurse, Cynthia Markus, MD, President, Washington State Medical Association, Duane French, disability rights leader, Not Dead Yet Washington, Rose Crumb, RN, hospice nurse, founder Volunteer Hospice of Clallam County, David Cortinas, publisher of LaVoz Histpanic Paper, Linda Seamon, MD, FAAHPM, Connecticut Knights of Columbus, Knights of Columbus, Washington State Catholic Conference, Archdiocese of Seattle, Catholic Health Association, United States Conference of Catholic Bishops

Table created by author from each bill's legislative history.

Table 2.3 Recent Utilization Demographics

	Oregon[i]			*Washington*[ii]	*Netherlands*[iii]	*Belgium*[iv]
	2016	*1998–2015*	*Total*	*2016*	*2016*	*2015*
Physician-prescribed substances (Death with Dignity)	133	994	1,127	240	216	2022
Physician-administred substances	0	0	0	0	5856	
Sex						
Male (%)	72 (54.1)	510 (51.3)	585 (51.6)	120 (50)	3130	2026 (51.3)
Female (%)	61 (45.9)	484 (48.7)	545 (48.4)	119 (50)	2961	1924 (48.7)
Race						
White (%)	127 (96.2)	956 (96.6)	1,083 (96.5)	232 (97)	NA	NA
African American (%)	0 (0.0)	1 (0.1)	1 (0.1)	All non-White	NA	NA
American Indian (%)	0 (0.0)	2 (0.2)	2 (0.2)	7 (3)	NA	NA
Asian (%)	2 (1.5)	13 (1.3)	15 (1.3)		NA	NA
Pacific Islander (%)	0 (0.0)	1 (0.1)	1 (0.1)		NA	NA
Other (%)	0 (0.0)	3 (0.3)	3 (0.3)		NA	NA
Two or more races (%)	1 (0.8)	4 (0.4)	5 (0.4)		NA	NA
Hispanic (%)	2 (1.5)	10 (1.0)	12 (1.1)		NA	NA
Unknown	1	4	5	0	NA	NA
Age						
<18 (%)					NA	0
18–34 (%)	1 (0.8)	8 (0.8)	9 (0.8)	6 (3)	NA	13 (0.03) (18–29)
35–44 (%)	1 (0.8)	23 (2.3)	24 (2.1)		NA	42 (1.1) (30–39)
45–54 (%)	6 (4.5)	64 (6.4)	70 (6.2)	12 (5)	NA	134 (3.4) (40–49)
55–64 (%)	18 (13.5)	206 (20.7)	224 (19.9)	53 (22)	NA	428 (10.8) (50–59)
65–74 (%)	52 (39.1)	289 (29.1)	341 (30.3)	59 (25)	NA	850 (21.5) (60–69)

(Continued)

Table 2.3 (Continued)

	Oregon[i]			*Washington*[ii]	*Netherlands*[iii]	*Belgium*[iv]
	2016	*1998–2015*	*Total*	*2016*	*2016*	*2015*
75–84 (%)	31 (23.3)	259 (26.1)	290 (25.7)	67 (28)	NA	1067 (27.0) (70–79)
≥85 (%)	24 (18.0)	145 (14.6)	169 (15)	42 (18)	NA	1416 (35.8) (80–100+)
Unknown					1	1
Education						
Less than high school (%)	5 (3.8)	58 (5.9)	63 (5.6)	10 (4)	NA	
High school graduate (%)	23 (17.4)	218 (22.1)	241 (21.5)	65 (27)	NA	
Some college (%)	38 (28.8)	261 (26.4)	299 (26.7)	84 (35)	NA	
Baccalaureate or higher (%)	66 (50.0)	450 (45.6)	516 (46.1)	77 (32)	NA	
Unknown				3(1)	NA	
Marital Status						
Married (including Registered Domestic Partners) (%)	62 (47.0)	449 (45.4)	511 (45.5)	105 (44)	NA	
Widowed (%)	26 (19.7)	232 (23.4)	258 (23.0)	47 (20)	NA	
Divorced (%)	36 (27.3)			65 (27)	NA	
Never married/single (%)	8 (6.1)	78 (7.9)	86 (7.7)	17 (7)	NA	
Unknown (%)	1	4	5	5 (1)	NA	
Disease profile						
Cancer (%)	105 (78.9)	767 (77.2)	872 (77.4)	184 (77)	4137	2675 (67.7)
Neuro-degenerative disease (including ALS)	9 (6.8)	80 (8.0)	89 (7.9)	18 (8)	411	274 (6.9)
Respiratory (%)	2 (1.5)	44 (4.4)	46 (4.1)	18 (8)	214	124 (3.1)
Cardiovascular (%)	9 (6.8)	26 (2.6)	35 (3.1)	14 (6)	315	205 (5.2)
Dementia			NA		141	
Psychiatric disorders (%)					60	124 (3.1)
HIV/AIDS (%)	0 (0.0)	10 (1.0)	10 (0.9)	NA	NA	
Combination of disorders	NA	NA	NA	NA	465	385 (9.7)

Other (including multi-factorial)	8 (6.0)	67 (6.7)	75 (6.7	5(2)	348	
Patient died at						
Home (patient, family, or friend) (%)	117 (88.6)	931 (94.0)	1,048 (93.4)	NA	NA	(44)
Long term care, assisted living or foster care facility (%)	9 (6.8)	46 (4.6)	55 (4.9)	NA	NA	12
Hospital (%)	3 (2.3)	1 (0.1)	4 (0.4)	NA	NA	42
Other (%)	3 (2.3)	12 (1.2)	15 (1.3)	NA	NA	
Unknown	1	4	5	NA	NA	

[i] Public Health Division, Center for Health Statistics, "Oregon Death with Dignity Act: Data Summary 2016," *Oregon Health Authority Public Health Division*, 2017, https://www.oregon.gov/oha/ph/ProviderPartnerResources/EvaluationResearch/DeathwithDignityAct/Documents/year19.pdf.

[ii] Washington State Department of Health, "Washington State 2016 Death with Dignity Act Report." *Center for Health Statistics*, 2017, https://www.doh.wa.gov/Portals/1/Documents/Pubs/422-109-DeathWithDignityAct2016.PDF.

[iii] Regional Euthanasia Review Committees (RTE). 2017. "Annual Report 2016." Regional Euthanasia Review Committees https://english.euthanasiecommissie.nl/the-committees/documents/publications/annual-reports/2002/annual-reports/annual-reports (August 5, 2018).

[iv] Federal Control and Evaluation Committee on Euthanasia, "Seventh Report to the Legislative Chambers (for the Years 2014 and 2015). *European Institute of Bioethics*, 2016, https://www.ieb-eib.org/en/pdf/20161008-en-synthese-rapport-euthanasie.pdf.

Data Sources: Public Health Division, Center for Health Statistics, "Oregon Death with Dignity Act: Data Summary 2016," *Oregon Health Authority Public Health Division*, 2017, https://www.oregon.gov/oha/ph/ProviderPartnerResources/EvaluationResearch/DeathwithDignityAct/Documents/year19.pdf; Washington State Department of Health, "Washington State 2016 Death with Dignity Act Report." *Center for Health Statistics*, 2017, https://www.doh.wa.gov/Portals/1/Documents/Pubs/422-109-DeathWithDignityAct2016.PDF; Regional Euthanasia Review Committees (RTE). 2017. "Annual Report 2016." Regional Euthanasia Review Committees https://english.euthanasiecommissie.nl/the-committees/documents/publications/annual-reports/2002/annual-reports/annual-reports (August 5, 2018); Federal Control and Evaluation Committee on Euthanasia, "Seventh Report to the Legislative Chambers (for the Years 2014 and 2015). *European Institute of Bioethics*, 2016, https://www.ieb-eib.org/en/pdf/20161008-en-synthese-rapport-euthanasie.pdf.

or have a domestic partner, and educated. In 2016, only seven of the 239 of the people who received prescriptions for lethal medications in Washington State were minority. These findings comport with public opinion that finds that whites are more inclined to support some circumstances that allow patients to die than minorities. Whites, who are much more likely to identify as Republican or Republican leaning than African Americans, Hispanics, and Asians, are less likely to support PAD legislation but are statistically more likely to take advantage of it.[36] Besides ethnicity, illness also contributes to PAD utilization decision making. Most patients who take death with dignity prescriptions are diagnosed with some form of terminal cancer and choose to die at home.

CONCLUSION

While the inclusion of an issue on a political party's platform may accelerate legislative responsiveness to them, this chapter reveals how policy entrepreneurs navigated the problem to eventually achieve legislative success. In the policy stream, promoting more widely accepted solutions, especially those that unequivocally denounced lingering eugenics themes was a start, but also building coalitions in the politics stream finally readied them for their window of opportunity creating two distinct paths to reform. The one path concentrates on protecting patient's rights to withdraw or refuse treatment and the second path establishes a right to initiate death. Growing national interest in living wills coupled with *Quinlin* created a "policy window" for the more conservative and political acceptable path that established a foundation for its most recent innovation, Physician Orders for Life-Sustaining Treatment (POLST). Then in 1997 Oregon voters approved the nation's first death with dignity law by ballot, establishing the more controversial path for what became known as the death with dignity movement. The law and its adoption would serve as the protype for aid in death activists in other states.

The unique political and religious conditions under which states adopt PAD sheds light on who supports and utilizes the laws. Democratic party control in state government and religiousity are strong indictors of policy adoption. While all residents in adopting states have the option to request lethal prescription drugs, minorities are statistically less likely to do so. Instead, aid in dying decendents are primarily married, educated, elderly, and white.

Policy entrepreneurs initiated the right to die movement but were not the only major contributors. The next chapter draws from the interest group literature to explore the conditions under which the two-founding assisted death interest groups—Euthanasia Society of America and the Hemlock Society—emerged and to trace their ongoing educational and legislative contributions to the right to die movement in the United States.

NOTES

1. Karen Quinlan survived the removal of the respirator and remained in a coma until her death in 1985.

2. California Safety Code. Part 1, division 7, chapter 3.9, sections 7185–7195.

3. Keene served the California State Assembly 1972–1978 and California State Senate, 1978–1992.

4. California Assembly Bill 3060.

5. Oregon Ballot Measure 16 (ORS 127.800-995).

6. Patients Rights Council, "Attempts to Legalize Euthanasia/Assisted-Suicide in the United States," *Patients Rights Council,* n.d., http://www.patientsrightscouncil.org/site/failed-attempts-usa/.

7. Gardner was aware Parkinson's disease was not included in the law. He succumbed to complications of Parkinson's in 2013 at the age of seventy-six (Yardley 2013).

8. In 2003, it changed its name to Oregon Death with Dignity but became Death with Dignity National Center the following year after merger with the California-based nonprofit. The headquarters for the new organization is Portland, Oregon (Death with Dignity, n.d.).

9. In part, the Act sought to amend Washington's Natural Death Act (70.122 RCW) by specifying the refusal of artificial nutrition and hydration machines to its general reference to "life-sustaining procedures (Daniel Hillyard and John Dombrink, *Dying Right: The Death with Dignity Movement* [New York: Routledge, 2001]).

10. According to the Death with Dignity website, the Yes on I-1000 raised $4,890,020, which also includes $300,000 from Governor Garner making him the largest single contributor to the campaign. Alternatively, opposition groups rose a little over a half of million dollars (see Ball 2017 for a more extensive discussion about death with dignity opposition group).

11. During the first decade of Oregon's Death with Dignity Act, 341 patients died from lethal prescriptions. Hal Bernton, "Washington's Initiative 1000 is Modeled on Oregon's Death with Dignity Act." *The Seattle Times,* October 13, 2008, http://www.seattletimes.com/seattle-news/washingtons-initiative-1000-is-modeled-on-oregonons-death-with-dignity-act/.

12. AB 1080 The Death with Dignity Act and AB 1310 The Death with Dignity Act were identical measures introduced in 1995 by assembly members Diane Martinez (D-Monterey Park) and Kerry Mazzoni (D-Novato), respectively. The bills, which mirrored Oregon's Death with Dignity law, did not gain a legislative hearing. In 1999, assembly member Dion Aroner (D-Berkeley) introduced AB 1592 The Death With Dignity Act, which passed the Assembly Judiciary and the Appropriations Committee but was pulled before reaching the floor for lack of votes and died in the 2000 session (Hillyard and Dombrink, *Dying Right: The Death with Dignity Movement*). Assembly member Patty Berg (D-Eureka, First District) introduced AB 654 Compassionate Choices Act in 2005, which quickly passed through committee but stalled on the floor.

Patty Berg (D-Eureka, First District) and Lloyd Levine (D-Van Nuys) introduced AB 651, the California Compassionate Choices Act in 2006. The Democratic-controlled Senate Judiciary Committee rejected it. When the measure was reintroduced as AB 374 California Compassionate Choices Act in 2007, it passed the Assembly Judiciary Committee and the Assembly Appropriations Committee, but it did not receive the necessary support to pass the measure through a full vote and was shelved.

13. Prior to the 2012 diagnosis, he had a small basal cell carcinoma removed from his ear in 2008, and a cancerous growth removed from his nose in 2011 (Patrick McGreevy, "After Struggling, Jerry Brown Makes Assisted Suicide Legal in California." *Los Angeles Times*, October 5, 2015, http://www.latimes.com/local/political/la-me-pc-gov-brown-end-of-life-bill-20151005-story.html.

14. ABX2-15 (AB 15) went into effect January 2016.

15. On June 9, 2016, the day the law took effect, groups including the Life Legal Defense Foundation and American Academy of Medical Ethics filed a lawsuit against the law because of its passage during a special session. California superior court Judge Daniel A. Ottolia overturned the bill May 2018 thus putting implementation of the law on hold until further notice but the Fourth District Court of Appeals in Riverside issued an immediate stay the following month reinstating the law. Opponents have until July 2 to file objections. Associated Press, "Death with Dignity Law Has Second Life as Court Grants Stay." *CBS Sacramento*, June 15, 2018, http://sacramento.cbslocal.com/2018/06/15/death-with-dignity-stay-granted/.

16. Connecticut (HB 6928, SB 334), New Mexico (SB 446), New York (S 1683, S 5024-A, A 6333), Maine (HB 552), Maryland (HB 933, HB 474), Massachusetts (H 3173), Rhode Island (SB 2985), Vermont (H 335), and Wisconsin (AB 174, SB 90).

17. J. Adrian Stanley, "Right-to-die Legislation Stirs Up Strong Feelings, Concerns." *Colorado Springs Independent,* February 4, 2015, https://www.csindy.com/coloradosprings/right-to-die-legislation-stirs-up-strong-feelings-concerns/Content?oid=2996672.

18. Clay Evans, "Clay Evans: Behand the Killing of Death with Dignity." *Daily Camera,* February 23, 2015, http://www.dailycamera.com/columnists/ci_27585622/clay-evans-behind-killing-death-dignity.

19. Death with Dignity National Center, "Colorado." *Death with Dignity,* n.d., https://www.deathwithdignity.org/states/colorado/.

20. David Kelly, "In Colorado, Terminally Ill Man's Public Letter Spurs Lawmakers to Act." *Los Angeles Times,* December 26, 2014, http://www.latimes.com/nation/la-na-colorado-right-to-die-20141226-story.html; Charles Selsberg, "Please, I Want to Die." *The Denver Post*, February 27, 2014, https://www.denverpost.com/2014/02/27/please-i-want-to-die/.

21. Ballotpedia, "Colorado End of Life Options Act, Proposition 106 (2016)." *Ballotpedia,* n.d., https://ballotpedia.org/Colorado_End_of_Life_Options_Act,_Proposition_106_(2016).

22. Death with Dignity, "District of Columbia." *Death with Dignity*, n.d., https://www.deathwithdignity.org/states/district-of-columbia/.

23. Richard J Rosendall, "Building on Victory: A 2015 Special Election Guide to LGBT Issues in Washington, DC." *Gay and Lesbian Activists Alliance of Washington, DC*, March 4, 2016, http://glaa.org/archive/2016/buildingonvictory2016.pdf.

24. DC Law 21-182.

25. In addition to its three original Republican co-sponsors in the House and Republican three sponsors in the Senate, 55 Republican Representatives joined HJ

Res.27 55/SJ Res. 4—Disapproving the action of the District of Columbia Council in approving the Death with Dignity Act of 2016.

26. Mary Cheh, "Statement on Amendment Seeking Repeal of the District's Death with Dignity Law." Mary Cheh, Ward 3 DC Council, n.d., www.marycheh.com/release/statement-on-amendment-seeking-repeal-of-the-districts-death-with-dignity-law/.

27. Mikaela Lefrak, "Trump Budget Aims to Block Funding for DC Death with Dignity Law." *WAMU 88.5*, May 23, 2017, www.wamu.org/story/17/05/23/trump-budget-aims-block-funding-d-c-death-dignity-law/.

28. "Norton to Host Press Conference with Mayor Bowser and National Organizations to Defend DC Home Rule from FY 19 Appropriations Riders, Wednesday." *Congresswoman Eleanor Holmes Norton Representing the District of Columbia*, April 30, 2018, https://norton.house.gov/media-center/press-releases/norton-to-host-press-conference-with-mayor-bowser-and-national-3.

29. Death with dignity was not proposed in 2000.

30. Hawaii Right to Life, National Right to Life, the Respect Life Office of the Catholic Diocese of Hawaii, and the Hawaii Partnership for Appropriate Compassionate Care were among the coalition of organization that lobbied against HB 2487.

31. In 2017, the Senate introduced the following bills: SB 1129 "Hawai'i Death with Dignity Act," SB 357 "Hawai'i Patient Choice at End of Life Act." That same year, the House introduced HB 201 "Hawai'i Patient Choice at End of Life Act," HB 150 "Hawai'i End of Life Options Act", HB 550 "Hawai'i Death with Dignity Act." In addition to HB 2739 "Hawai'i Our Care Our Choice Act," the House introduced HB 2218 "Hawai'i Voluntary Assisted Dying Act," HB 2736 "Hawai'i Our Care Our Choice Act," and the Senate introduced SB 2727 "Hawai'i Medical Aid in Dying Act" in 2018.

32. Jim Mendoza, "After Two Decades of Debate, Medical 'Aid in Dying' Bill Signed into Law." *Hawaii News Now*, April 5, 2018, www.hawaiinewsnow.com/story/37890922/hawaii-governor-set-to-sign-medical-aid-in-dying-bill.

33. Pew Research Center Religion and Public Life, "Religious Landscape Study." *Pew Research Center*, n.d., http://www.pewforum.org/religious-landscape-study/.

34. Although several evangelical Protestant denominations oppose policies that control death, the Episcopal, Unitarian Universalist, Methodist, Presbyterian, and Quaker churches accept stopping medical treatment when it no longer improves a person's quality of life. The United Church of Christ and the Methodist Churches on the West Coast are the only evangelical Protestant churches that support the right-to-die.

35. Jim Norman, "The Religious Regions of the US." *Gallup*, April 6, 2018, https://news.gallup.com/poll/232223/religious-regions.aspx; Jeffrey M. Jones, "Tracking Religious Affiliation, State by State." *Gallup,* June 22, 2004, https://news.gallup.com/poll/12091/tracking-religious-affiliation-state-state.aspx.

36. Pew Research Center, "Wide Gender Gap, Growing Educational Divide in Voters' Party Identification." *Pew Research Center*, March 20, 2018, http://www.people-press.org/2018/03/20/1-trends-in-party-affiliation-among-demographic-groups/.

Chapter 3

Interest Groups

Despite their conflicting policy goals, the blending of *eugenics* during the Progressive Era enhanced the need for aid in dying mobilization. In the 1910s, Dr. Harry J. Haiselden's candor about committing infantcide represents one of the more notable representations of society's misguided understanding about the two causes. Following the delivery of their son, whom he diagnosed as a baby with physical defects including most urgently, the absence of an anal aperture, Dr. Haiselden advised the Bollingers not to have the life-saving artificial anus constructed. Baby Boy Bollinger died five days later. From a personal standpoint, the Bollinger case provided Dr. Haiselden a personal platform to publicly advocate for withholding treatment for defective infants. However, his eugenic characterization of hastening death had a much deeper and far lasting impact on the right to die movement.[1] While Dr. Haiselden's sensationalized linkages between eugenics and aid in dying reflect Progressive Era thinking that had yet to make distinctions between aid in dying and murder, Dr. Haiselden and the Bollinger case publicly solidified their union.

In 1938, New York clergyman and author Charles Francis Potter and social elite Ann Mitchell established Euthanasia Society of America (ESA) in New York, to promote the legalization of aid in dying and to disseminate information about and to inform the public about aid in dying. The internal clash between its aid in dying mission and its members' focus on eugenics resulted in a series of spin-offs, mergers, name and a mission changes, and only one legislative proposal during its seventy-year tenure.

The Euthanasia Educational Council (EEC) formed as a branch of the ESA in the late 1960s and began to promote healthcare advance directives. After several name changes in the mid-1970s, aid in dying advocacy members increasingly doubted EECs (now known as Care for Dying) interest painless death policy reform, which was ESA's initial mission. Then in 1980, British-born author Derek Humphry and his second wife, Ann Wickett, started Hemlock Society in Santa Monica, California. Hemlock Society would also generate a series of spin-offs as well as leadership and experience significant upheaval. Yet its efforts resulted, both directly and indirectly, in the adoption of PAD statutes in seven jurisdictions—Oregon, Washington State, Vermont, California, Colorado, the District of Columbia, and Hawaii.

During one of the most vibrant and active periods for interest group activity in national politics, mobilization for aid in dying lagged other prominent Progressive Era movements. This raises some questions: Why did it take activists so long to establish the first interest group devoted to aid in dying, and what explains the two major organizations' diverging outcomes? The answer to the first question requires a general understanding of group mobilization; the interest group literature offers three schools of thought on this subject. Early interest group scholars such as Truman embraced pluralism by explaining mobilization as an organic occurrence that responds to changes in the policy environment. By the mid-1960s, Olson's transactional/economic perspective disputed this assertion, claiming that political interest alone induces group activity by contending that without sufficiently incentivizing participation, individuals will always choose to remain free riders. Since the mid-1980s, however, interest group scholars have embraced a neo-pluralist perspective that recognizes the various constraints in a state's political environment that affect mobilization of activists and their ability to influence on policymaking. For example, the involvement, and more importantly, the impact of interest groups in the states is thought to be inversely related to the strength of the parties in the states—stronger, more competitive political parties result in weaker interest groups.

The question as to the diverging outcomes of the ESA and Hemlock Society, the two most prominent organizations in the right to die movement, lies in their history and the evolution attitudes, ideas, and debates among their leaders and members, which influenced the discourse on aid in dying and legislative progress in the United States. The chapter relies on the interest group literature to examine the factors that led to the creation of each group and the internal and external factors that shaped their influence on policy reform.

THE FORMATION OF THE EUTHANASIA SOCIETY OF AMERICA

For most of the movement's history, physicians have collectively remained quiet about their position on aid in dying. Even though PAD occurs outside of the glare of the public or lawmakers' attention, public pronouncements about offering aid to hasten death challenged the medical profession's enduring commitment to save lives, which was the position championed by medical associations' for decades. Charles Killick Millard, a retired public health physician in Leicester, England, was an exception. Millard, well-known for views on birth control and overcrowding underpinned by eugenic ideas about good breeding, spent the years between 1931 and 1935 gathering a group of physicians, clerics, scientists, and writers to establish the Voluntary Euthanasia Legalization Society (VELS) that persists in England today as Dignity in Dying. The following year, the group managed to get an aid in dying bill introduced into Great Britain's House of Lords, but the measure was defeated 35 to 14. Still, their approach provided a model for advocates in the United States to emulate.

In contrast to physicians, the public was more interested and tolerant of aid in dying, particularly during the 1930s. Coverage of *mercy killing* cases at the time focused on victims' personal suffering and the grim choices that their accused killers faced. A national poll conducted in the late 1930s found that almost half of Americans favored aid in dying for deformed or mentally disabled infants and 37 percent favored it for terminally ill adults. A 1939, *Time* magazine article estimated that *mercy killings* occurred roughly once a week in the United States.

In 1936, Ann Mitchell, a wealthy, married New Yorker, attended a lecture on aid in dying by Charles Francis Potter. Already familiar with VELS, she approached him about establishing a similar organization with her in the United States. Potter had been ordained a Baptist minister in 1908 and, subsequently, became a pastor of the Unitarian Church in 1913. During the 1920s, he advocated for many progressive social reforms, including eugenics sterilization but did not public endorse aid in dying until two years before cofounding ESA. He founded the First Humanist Society of New York in in 1929. Potter championed PAD as well as hastening death for defective babies and those with incurable mental illness.

Mitchell had been drawn to PAD advocacy by her own mental health issues. She was institutionalized in an asylum as a patient for two years between 1934 and 1936 and came out convinced that mental illness is a genetic disease and that, in most cases, psychiatry does more harm than good. She advocated for the killings of incurable mental asylum patients and defective babies as the only solution for problems such as her own.

ESA began as the National Society for the Legalization of Euthanasia (NSLE) on January 16, 1938. Founding members comprised a list of Manhattan's educated elite, including Robert Frost, Somerset Maugham, Sherwood Anderson, Fannie Hurst, Rex Stout, Max Eastman, physician Walter Alvarez, and physiologist Walter B. Cannon. The advisory council included a few of the most prominent names in the eugenics movement including Henry Goodard, Arthur Estabrook (biologist), Albert Wiggam, author of the *New Decalogue of Society*, and Leon F. Whitney, author of *The Case for Sterilization*. Publicly, the organization promoted "the lawful termination of human life by painless means to avoid unnecessary suffering and under adequate safeguards" but privately, enduring ties to eugenics complicated its message and stymied its growth and influence.[2]

The Clash between Individual Beliefs and Shared Interests

Its focus on the various external factors that led to mobilization makes the pluralist perspective a viable explanation for ESA's formation; however, as Olson argues, this perspective assumes that the interests of rational, self-interested actors mirror the group's shared interest. The transactional/economic perspective, which stems from Olson's collective action theory, contends that the costs (e.g., time, opportunity, financial) associated with cooperation for the collective good makes inducements essential for group membership. Wilson expounds on the transactional/economic perspective by identifying four categories of incentives that interest groups can offer to induce membership—informational, material, solidary, and purposive benefits.[3] In the early development stage of an interest group, leadership chooses its organizational and financial strategy. The source of an interest group's financial support (either from its niche constituency or the policy community) determines whether it will concentrate on an "inside" or "outside" strategy. An inside strategy calls for close ties with political leaders who play the major role in providing the resources necessary to sustain the group and its influence or function while an outside strategy concentrates on eliciting public interest and support to sustain the group.

For much of its history, differing opinions about eugenics as well the role of women in the organization eroded ESA's credibility as an aid in dying advocacy organization in the press, which caused ongoing feuds within the organization. Potter left the organization in 1938, citing the need to devote more time to earning an income and to the Humanist Society. Neurologist Foster Kennedy's two-month tenure as president illuminated the disconnect between members' personal beliefs and the organization's mission to advocate and inform the public about merciful death. As Kennedy explained to the *New York Times* in 1939, his interest in hastening death focused exclusively on ending the lives of the severely mentally disabled, whom he described as "nature's mistakes." Ending the lives of those suffering from terminal illness, or "normal adults, who have become ill" puts too much faith in doctors who, he believed, frequently errored in prognosis and diagnosis. The press and other physicians condemned both Kennedy and ESA in response.

Mitchell also publicly espoused support for eugenics. She described World War II as an opportunity for "biological house cleaning," describing euthanizing "the insane, feeble-minded monstrosities" in society as the only way to create a society strong enough to defeat Nazi Germany (55). While these statements alienated members and drew criticism, the fact that she was speaking in public at all drew criticism from those who thought women should remain in supporting roles. Mitchell nonetheless served as secretary and board member until her death in 1942.

Mitchell was also ESA's financier. Her contributions did not support any personnel salaries or the ability to keep the organization's Manhattan office open five days a week but sustained the organization to the extent that identifying inducements to attract new members remained a low organizational priority for many decades. By the end of the 1930s, membership was stagnant at around 200 people.

From an organizational standpoint, however, ESA had the resources to attempt outsider and insider strategies. Member Rabbi Sidney Goldstein was instrumental in ESA's pursuit of an outside strategy that concentrated on bringing public awareness to aid in dying which led to the change in name from National Society for the Legalization of Euthanasia to Euthanasia Society of America May 3, 1938. Goldstein saw the name change as a way to promote the educational component of the group's purpose. Proponents of the original name, which had been selected in part because of the influence of VELS, believed that public acceptance would follow legislative success. Notwithstanding Goldstein's victory, the organization remained divided on the extent to which the organization should dedicate itself to legalization.

ESA also attempted an insider strategy during its first year by a drafting an aid in dying bill and seeking political support for it from state legislators. The next internal battle ESA had to navigate was the eugenicists' members insistence on including the aging, insane, and disabled infants and children. Their opponents won out, however, and the draft legislation ultimately included a series of safeguards: It called on the state to permit terminally ill patients who were at least twenty-one years old and "of sound mind" to petition the court in writing for permission to seek medication with which to hasten their own death. A court proceeding would follow that would involve an attending doctor, witnesses, and a court-appointed committee that would verify the petitioners claim before the patient could administer a life-ending drug. The Roman Catholic Church's hard line stance on hastening death, coupled with its political and cultural dominance in New York in the 1930s blocked the bill, however, and it was never introduced in New York or any other state.

The Implications of World War II for ESA from the Neo-Pluralist Perspective

The number of national interest groups proliferated in Washington, DC during the 1960s and 1970s, and in the ensuing decades interest group scholars began to question the transactional/economic perspective and consider new explanations for group mobilization. The neo-pluralist perspective disputes Olson's collective action theory and therefore the notion that mobilization arises exclusively from intra-organizational forces. It focuses instead on the various actors, institutions, and events that influence group mobilization. ESA members' public flirtations with eugenics had a haunting effect on the organization during and in the decades following World War II. The interconnection between voluntary and involuntary death that played out during the war not only tarnished ESA as organization, it had a lasting effect on the right to die movement and its advocacy for hastening death for the terminally ill.

Whereas Mitchell saw World War II as an opportunity to frame eugenics as a national imperative, news of Nazi atrocities in the 1940s rendered any association with *euthanasia*, including the word itself, politically toxic. The United States entered the war at the end of 1943 and Americans were urged to denounce the Third Reich. Nevertheless, Potter and birth control advocate Jean Burnett Tompkin formed a committee in that year to draft a bill that would legalize state-sponsored death for "idiots, imbecils, and congenital monstrosities." Nothing became of their efforts.

By the end of the 1940s, ESA's new leaders, president Robert Latou Dickinson, the former chairmen of the American Medical Association and then-vice president of Planned Parenthood, and executive vice president Eleanor Dwight Jones, former president of the Birth Control League from 1929 to 1935, began to accept that without any effort to implement an outside strategy, even if only to draw legislative support, their policy initiatives would continue to fail.[4] In a rare display of policy advocacy for PAD, in 1947, ESA formed a committee of doctors called the "Committee of 1776 Physicians for Legalization of Voluntary Euthanasia in New York," petitioned every state legislature to introduce a bill that would permit PAD for the terminally ill over the age of twenty-one. Though signed by over 1,000 doctors, the mood in the country, and particularly within the medical profession and the Catholic Church, remained hostile toward PAD legalization. In 1950, the American Medical Association (AMA), issued a statement denouncing aid in dying and threating punishment for any physicians who publicly defied the organization's stance. The professional threat that the AMA represented in terms of patient referrals, malpractice liability protections, and hospital privileges pushed New York doctors away from the issue. When the committee circulated a similar petition in New Jersey in 1957, the Archdiocese of

Newark went a step further by publishing the names of the 166 signatories of the petition sent to the members of the New Jersey legislature in the newspaper. Many of the signatories claimed that they had never signed the petition or that they had not fully understood what it meant. Between the Archdiocese of New York and strong public opposition from Medical Society of New Jersey, the effort came to an abrupt end.

In 1950, two high-profile *mercy killing* cases in the New England states provided opportunities for ESA to establish new chapters. A twenty-one-year-old Connecticut college student named Carol Paight fatally shot her father, a police officer, with his revolver in the hospital after learning about his incurable cancer. Eleanor Dwight Jones and Charles Potter assisted prominent local activists in the birth control movement as well as renowned Yale University figures, in establishing the Voluntary Euthanasia Society of Connecticut (VESC) to support Ms. Paight, who was ultimately acquitted by reason of temporary insanity.[5]

While VESC would ultimately introduce a bill to permit PAD to the Connecticut legislature that gained some support before its demise, ESA's support for another high-profile defendant backfired.[6] Dr. Hermann Sander's *mercy killing* trial was the first case of a doctor on trial for hastening the death of a patient. Sander had a groundswell of support from neighbors and renowned aid in dying activists at his trial in New Hampshire. Heavily swayed by the defense's argument that the patient was already deceased before the injection, a jury of "twelve middle-aged and elderly men" found him not guilty. Sander refused to join ESA in publicly advocating for aid in dying.[7] In the end, Eleanor Dwight Jones's efforts to start an ESA chapter in New Hampshire proved unsuccessful. Despite repeated attempts to draw public support and attract political allies who are will to introduce their policies, ESA's reform efforts during the 1940s and much of the 1950s demonstrated how ill-prepared they were for the ideological, social, medical, and religious forces aligned against them.

ESA's Shift in Policy and Philosophy, 1950s–1970s

Changes in demography, medical technology, and the The Catholic Church in the late 1950s gave rise to a new policy direction. ESA became a major resource for information about on death and dying during the 1960s and 1970s. Its spin off organization, Euthanasia Educational Fund, bolstered membership and national recognition by disseminating copies of living wills.

World War II was but one of several external forces to affect ESA. Technological innovations in medicine such as respirators, artificial feeding machines, and antibiotics helped to treat many more common diseases leading to considerably fewer deaths from pneumonia, tuberculosis, and influenza. However, an increase in the senior citizen population also brought about a growing number of deaths from chronic diseases such as cancer. The rise of the hospice and palliative care movement in the 1950s struck a blow to the right to die movement by demonstrating that controlling pain for terminal patients lessens the need for aid in dying. However its individualistic approach to caring for and restoring the dignity of dying patients offered another perspective to the national discourse on death. Then on February 24, 1957, Pope Pius XII, announced that the Catholic doctrine permitted terminally ill patients to refuse life-sustaining treatment and to request its withdrawal.[8] The Catholic Church's tolerence of passive methods of hasten death presented the persistently divided ESA with the opportunity to work toward the members' shared goal of enhancing ESA's relevance in the movement beyond Manhattan, even if that meant changing its mission to supporting more conservative end of life policies and giving up its policymaking aspirations information dissemination.

At the end of the 1950s, ESA was on life support. It had only added about a hundred or so paying members since the late 1930s and with a reputation as a radical group, mainstream magazines such as *Harper*'s and *Atlantic Monthly* would no longer publish ESA advertisements. In 1962, ESA's lawyer and first female president, Pauline Taylor, sought heroic measures to revive the organization. She decided to revive the outside strategy by concentrating on education to change public opinion, by establishing a tax-exempt charitable organization initially named the Euthanasia Educational Fund (EEF), but renamed the Euthanasia Education Council (EEC) in 1967. ESA had finally become a nationally recognized and sought after right to die organization.[9] ESA members collectively agreed to shift their focus to policies the Pope had declared acceptable by changing the organizations' purpose and goals to promote a "rights" message through a speakers bureau, seminar sponsorship, and television and radio show appearances.[10]

Even with its success in academic circles, as the transactional/economic perspective contends, ESA would need to attract new members to remain solvent. In 1967, Luis Kutner, cofounder of Amnesty International of London, presented the idea of the living will to ESA and by 1969, an EEF committee drafted and dissiminated 5,000 copies in less than nine months. Requests for copies often led to membership or donations; the organization's annual budget grew from $12,000 in 1967 to over $400,000 ten years later. By 1975 ESA had 70,000 members.

Although many of its leaders abandoned aid in dying reform, a growing number of members wanted to continue the fight. In 1974, the reformers regained control. As the new president, Joseph Fletcher was determined to reestablish ESA in the battle for aid in dying reform. The organization became the Society for the Right to Die (SRD) to officially purge any lingering associations with eugenics from its name and approach.[11] EEC became Concern for Dying (CFD) in 1978 and distanced itself from SRD's focus on aid in dying. Infighting about the $1 million Hugh Moore's estate left to the foundation, as well as the diverging interests between the two organizations, led to their official split in 1979.[12]

The Final Years of ESA's Legacy

As the continuum of advance directives continued to expand in the 1980s, the more radical Hemlock Society on the west coast increasingly became the leader in PAD advocacy in the United States. CFD remained committed to its educational pursuits, and SRD was divided over whether to pursue PAD legislation. The merger of the two organizations signaled the end of any aid in dying consideration and thus the exit of ardent aid in dying advocates. Although the new direction attracted grant funding from the Robert Wood Johnson Foundation, the final iteration of the group, Last Acts Partnerships, would unceremoniously end in 2004 and thus ending ESA's nearly seventy-year history.

Upheaval continued in the 1990s. While Hemlock's publications and ballot initiative campaigns began to eclipse the once prominent right to die groups, CFD and SRD decided to pool their resources for survival. Yet, before a merger could occur, SRD's most vocal aid in dying advocate members were either voted off the board of directors or resigned. CFD and SRD merged and became the National Council for Death and Dying (NCDD) in 1991. It was renamed Choice in Dying six months later.[13] The organization positioned itself as a patients' rights organization and devoted itself to promoting individual choice at the end of life by continuing CFD's educational and advocacy work, which helped it draw funding support. The organization changed its name again in 2001 to Partnership for Caring, Inc. (PFC), and distanced itself from the topic of aid in dying to concentrate on advance directives and improvement of care for the terminally ill. In part, through a major grant from the Robert Wood Johnson Foundation (RWJR) to manage the foundation's Last Acts program, it established an office in Washington, DC.[14] The turn against legalization of PAD was complete as the organization devoted itself to disseminating language for advanced medical directives and offering assistance to individuals dealing with end of life issues through a crisis and information hotline.[15] In 2004, PFC became the Last Acts Partnership, but it was gone less than a year later, due to "unexplained financial anomalies." RWJF shut down the website, thus ending ESA's legacy.

HEMLOCK SOCIETY'S ORIGINS

While the path to PAD reform in the United States in the 1970s led exclusively to living will laws, the decriminalization of aid in dying in the Netherlands renewed optimism for reformers around the world. The process began in 1971 when Jean Humphry asked her husband, British journalist Derek Humphry, to help her end her life before she succumbed to inoperable breast cancer. He complied four years later, mixing poison with coffee at her request. In 1978, he published a memoir about it: *Jean's Way: A Love Story*. The book was a bestseller in Britain and it reignited the aid in dying debate.[16] It galvanized PAD advocates in the United States who were already dissatisfied with ESA's lack of focus on reform. Humphry moved to California and after a brief stint with the *Los Angeles Times*, gave up journalism in 1980 and founded the Hemlock Society with his second wife, Ann Wickett, in his garage in Santa Monica. Its mission was twofold—to disseminate information about how the terminally ill can peacefully end their lives and to advocate for legalizing PAD.

"Final Exit" and Hemlock's Outside Strategy

According to the transactional/economic perspective, whether an interest group employs an inside or outside strategy and the types of benefits offered depends on its source of financial support. ESA's extraordinary ability to financially sustain itself for decades enabled the organization to explore both strategies without needing to pander to members or elected officials. Without benefactor-members, however, the grassroots Hemlock Society needed to select a strategy that would provide the financial foundation to pursue its policy and educational goals while also increasing membership. Humphry's initial reluctance to share specific details about the lethal cocktail of drugs that ended his first wife's life and how he acquired them in *Jean's Way* meant Hemlock Society already had individuals interested in his cause and a potential informational benefit to offer. Hemlock Society received a bevy of desperate personal letters seeking this information. The English and Scottish Voluntary Euthanasia Societies (known today as EXIT) had jointly published aid in dying guides in the 1970s, and the demand for a similar guide in United States was strong. Hemlock Society published its first guide, *Let Me Die before I Wake: Hemlock's Book of Self-Deliverance for the Dying* combined personal accounts with instruction on how to end one's life. The popularity of the book rapidly drew members, donations, and extensive media to attention to the organization. Humphry's 1991 follow up publication, *Final Exit*, provides readers with practical information about painlessly ending life including methods, avoiding legal issues, and how to identify doctors willing to write lethal prescriptions. For example, the book explains, "Physicians will sometimes write out prescriptions for the lethal doses if the patient asks by name for a specific drug in a sizable amount. It is part of the code in which the doctor is thinking: 'I know you might use this for suicide, but don't tell me'" (114). Within six months, *Final Exit* had hit the top of the *New York Times* bestseller list and it remained on the list for eighteen weeks. Hemlock Society had twelve full-time employees, more than eighty chapters around the country, and 57,000 members. It produced a newsletter, *Hemlock Quarterly*, with 40,000 readers.[17] To actively pursue its political goals, Hemlock founded Americans Against Human Suffering (AAHS) under the leadership of Robert Risley in 1986.

The Political Forces Leading to the Legalization of Physician Aid in Dying in Oregon

The neo-pluralist perspective acknowledges the importance of an interest group's financial and organizational strategies to its sustainability but devotes more attention to examining key actors and constraints in the political environment that directly affects a group's policymaking influence. Political parties' avoidance of the right to die debate essentially created a dynamic where, even when there were signs that public opinion favored aid in dying reform, legislators felt that bill sponsorship carried political risk. Prior to Humphry's involvement in aid in dying policymaking, it was generally accepted that reform depended on the receptiveness of legislators as gatekeepers. Aware of the political obstacles that existed in state legislatures, Hemlock Society and its offshoot groups pioneered a lobbying strategy that focused on citizen-centric policymaking institutions—the ballot initiative process and state courts—to adopt and protect aid in dying legislation. In 2013, aid in dying interest groups and lawmaker worked together to get death with dignity legislation enacted.

The Ballot Initiative Campaigns

AAHS launched its first ballot initiative in California, the "Humane and Dignified Death Act," in 1992. Following two unsuccessful attempts at gathering the requisite number of signatures, Humphry decided to move Hemlock's national headquarters from Los Angeles to Eugene, Oregon to concentrate on introducing measures in Washington State and Oregon.

The change in venue provided some measure of success. With the assistance of the former leader of the Washington State Hemlock chapter Ralph Mero, a Unitarian minister, and his organization Washington Citizens for Death and Dignity (WCDD), AAHS gathered the signatures necessary to get

Initiative 119, "The Death with Dignity Act" on the ballot in Washington State in 1991.[18] The measure would have decriminalized "aid in dying" for terminally ill patients by physicians. *Final Exit* had recently released to considerable fanfare in the state. However, two *mercy killing* cases in the state involving Dr. Jack Kevorkian as well as media attention to co-founder Ann Wickett's suicide following her divorce from Humphry raised enough questions about potential abuse to cause the measure's rejection.[19]

AAHS had become Californians against Human Suffering. It proposed Initiative 119 under the label Proposition 161 in California in 1992. The ballot measure failed by the same measure in California as it had in Washington State.

THE OREGON DEATH WITH DIGNITY LAW, MEASURE 16 (1994, 1997)

Despite a well-funded opposition campaign by the Roman Catholic Church, Ballot Measure 16, the "Oregon Death with Dignity Act," proposed by Hemlock of Oregon's political action committee, Oregon Right to Die passed in 1994 by a margin of 51 to 49 percent. The measure permits physicians to prescribe a fatal dose of medication to patients who met a host of preconditions, including having less than six months to live following the approval of two physicians, although patients had to administer the fatal dose themselves. Shortly after its passage, however, US District Court Judge Michael R. Hogan issued a restraining order and injunction to halt its implementation. The following year, the Oregon Death with Dignity Legal Defense and Education Center (formerly known as Californians against Human Suffering) was established to defend Measure 16. Nonetheless, Judge Hogan ruled that the measure violated the Equal Protection Clause of the US Constitution and made the injunction on implementation of the Act permanent.

To bury the Death with Dignity Act, the Oregon Catholic Conference lobbied the state legislature to introduce a bill to repeal, refer, delay or alter it. HB 2954 passed the Oregon State legislature and was then referred to voters as a referendum. On November 4, 1997, Measure 51, which would have repealed the Oregon Death with Dignity Act 1994, became law on October 27, 1997.[20] Once again, the law faced judicial scrutiny, this time led by US Attorney General John Ashcroft, who alleged that the law violated the Controlled Substances Act of 1970 and threated to revoke the medical licenses of physicians who prescribed lethal dosages to terminally ill patients. In a 6 to 3 decision, the US Supreme Court in *Gonzales v. Oregon* ruled that Attorney General John Ashcroft's directive overstepped his authority and determinations of whether a particular medical practice serves a legitimate purpose does not rest with the Attorney General, thus easing the path for states to legalize aid in dying.[21]

MICHIGAN'S LEGALIZATION OF LETHAL MEDICATION TO TERMINALLY ILL, PROPOSAL B (1998)

Former Michigan pathologist Dr. Jack Kevorkian's participation in the deaths of 130 willing participants in Michigan in the 1990s drew national attention to the right to die debate. In 1998, a group called Merian's Friends decided to revive Jack Kevorkian's 1994 failed ballot initiative campaign, "Prescribing Medication to End Life," Question 2, which sought to amend Michigan's Constitution establishing a right to aid in death.[22] Led by Ed Pierce, a retired doctor from Ann Arbor, Michigan, Merian's Friends put the measure known as Proposal B on the November ballot.[23] Polling data collected July of that year shows that 56 percent of Michigan voters supported the idea of reform. However, Merian's Friends had spent roughly $800,000 on getting the measure on the ballot, which left approximately $200,000 to rally support. Its opposition, Citizens for Compassionate Care, spent millions attacking the initiative through radio and television ads,[24] including $3.4 million alone from Catholic organizations, including the Michigan Catholic Conference.[25] The 12,000-word initiative caused voters to shift their attention away from the notion "hastening death" to the legal and practical implications of such a law in a state with a significant number of uninsured residents. Simply put, the grassroots organization lacked sophistication and political savvy to secure a legislative victory. The movement suffered a crushing defeat—71 percent to 29 percent[26]

MAINE PHYSICIAN-ASSISTED DEATHS FOR TERMINALLY ILL ADULTS, QUESTION 1 (2000)

While Hemlock Society and CID concentrated on improving the public's perception of physician assisted death, the Oregon Death with Dignity Legal Defense Fund and Education Center (ODLDEC) remained at the forefront of the legislative battle for legalization across states.[27] Following a series of failed legislative proposals in Maine in 1995, 1996, and 1997, in 2000, ODLDEC funded a ballot campaign that put Question 1, "Maine Death with Dignity Act" before voters by referendum. Maine's health care delivery system was in crisis at the time, and health care was considered an unaffordable luxury. Maine was ranked last in the US for hospice use and was one of six states that did not provide a hospice benefit for the poor through Medicaid.[28] Many voters saw aid in dying as vital given their dependence on Medicaid which would cover the cost of the prescription as it had in Oregon. In addition to raising doubts about the effectiveness of death with dignity in

Oregon, opposition groups portrayed the involvement of the national right to die movement as a political ploy. Even though the local aid in dying advocacy group, Mainers for Death with Dignity, organized the initiative and led the campaign, their reliance on out-of-state groups and individual donors for support was dismissed as a political move by the right to die movement to impose their national agenda on the state.[29] The measure suffered a narrow defeat by a 51 to 41 margin, a vote difference of only 6,000 votes statewide.

THE MASSACHUSETTS "DEATH WITH DIGNITY" INITIATIVE, QUESTION 2 (2012)

In 2012, Dignity 2012, a fifteen-person coalition comprised of Harvard Medical School professors, a former chaplain, and the executive and field directors of the Massachusetts American Civil Liberties Union, petitioned to put Question 2 on the 2012 general election ballot in Massachusetts.[30] One of its more visible members, Marcia Angell, became personally involved in the movement when her father, Lester W. Angell, then 81 years old, ended his seven-year battle with prostate cancer on March 15, 1988, by administering a self-inflicted gunshot wound to the head. The physician, former editor-in-chief of the *New England Journal of Medicine*, and current corresponding member of the faculty of Global Health and Social Medicine, told the *Washington Post* in 2002, "if physician-assisted suicide had been available to my father, as it is the people of Oregon, I have no doubt he would have chosen a less violent and lonely death."[31]

Although nearly 40 percent Massachusetts voters identified as Catholic, most embraced the idea of adopting PAD. In fact, public opinion polls conducted in May, August, and September showed at least 60 percent or more support for the measure.[32] The Question 2 campaign received close to $1 million, mostly from the national movement organization Compassion and Choices Action Network and the Death with Dignity National Center with endorsements from Social Workers of Massachusetts, American Medical Women's Association, and American Medical Student Association. In the final weeks of the campaign, however, its opposition, which included the Boston Archdiocese, Massachusetts Medical Society, anti-abortion groups, and others, spent $5 million on TV and radio ads attacking the language of specific provisions, which led to voters narrowly rejecting the measure, 51.9 percent to 48.1 percent. According to Massachusetts law, petitioners must wait five years before putting the same measure on the ballot following a defeat. The waiting period expired in 2018.[33]

Lobbying the Courts

The intent of Mero's Compassion in Dying (CID), which he started in 1993, was to offer one-on-one consultation services by providing personal assistance with all aspects of ending one's life except providing or administering the lethal drugs.[34] He had not anticpated the constitutional challenge of states' anti-aid in dying statutes that would lead to the US Supreme Court's first decision on PAD. Mero's candor with the press about his involvement in 24 deaths in CID's first thirteen months of existence got the attention of Kathryn Tucker, a young Seattle lawyer, who encouraged Mero to protect himself from prosecution by challenging Washington State's anti-aid in dying law in court. Citing the abortion decision in *Planned Parenthood* of *Southeastern Pennsylvania v. Casey*, Federal District Judge Barbara Rothstein ruled in *Compassion in Dying v. State of Washington* that Fourteenth Amendment due process and equal protections should also exist for the terminally ill at the end their lives.[35] Despite a three-judge panel of the United States Circuit Court of Appeals for the Ninth Circuit reversing the decision a year later, the lower court's decision was re-endorsed and reinstated by the *en banc* appellate panel in 1996.[36] Later that year, the Supreme Court agreed to review *Compassion in Dying* along with a similar case Tucker filed on behalf of several physicians in New York State to challenge its anti-PAD law, which had also won its appeal in to the Second Circuit US Court of Appeals.[37] On its face, the US Supreme Court's unanimous decision in *Washington v. Glucksberg* indicates a strong stance against establishing a federal constitutional right to physician assisted death, but a closer examination of the separate and concurring opinions signals an interest in considering the issue in the future.[38]

THE VERMONT PATIENT CHOICE AND CONTROL AT THE END OF LIFE ACT (2013)

At the end of a nearly twenty-year struggle to pass PAD legislation in Vermont was a demonstration of collective action by the local aid in dying organization, the national movement, and for the first time, elected officials, that resulted in the enactment of Act 39, the "Vermont Patient Choice and Control at the End of Life Act" in 2013. However, before group mobilization in Vermont, Democratic Representative Dean Corren (P-Chittenden 7-3) introduced four aid in dying bills in the 1990s.[39]

In 2002, after years of legislative inactivity and personal experiences with relatives' and friends' painful death, a seventy-seven-year-old retired Vermont couple by the name of Richard "Dick" and Ginny Walters, along with a group of friends, most of whom were retired physicians, started Patient

Choices Vermont.[40] Over the next year, and with guidance from the Death with Dignity National Center, Patient Choice Vermont drafted a death with dignity bill based on the Oregon Death with Dignity Act and actively promoted the measure in the Vermont legislature, among voters, and through the local media. In 2003, 38 House members and 8 Senators sponsored S 112/H 318 Vermont Death with Dignity Act. Over the course of the next ten years, legislators repeatedly sponsored Patient Choice's bill with little progress until 2011 when Democratic Governor Peter Shumlin became the first candidate to add death with dignity to his campaign platform.[41] In January 2013, the Senate Committee on Health and Welfare introduced the bill and on May 20, 2013, Governor Shumlin signed Act 39 into law. It took effect immediately. In 2014, the governor acknowledged Patient Choices Vermont for their unwavering commitment to the adoption of the aid in dying law.[42] Dick's comments on his organization's website state that the law's passage had brought him and "many Vermonters . . . peace of mind knowing that if someday in the future my suffering becomes intolerable, I will have choice and control. We all deserve tranquility and choice at the end of our lives."[43] A year later, Dick used the law he created to end his life after a rapid decline in health from lung cancer.[44]

CONCLUSION

The three prominent interest group perspectives not only provide a framework to understand the internal and external forces that affect interest groups' ability to attract and sustain their membership and influence public policy, but also illuminates their contributions to the right to die movement in the United States. The pervasiveness of eugenic thought in American society during and in the decades following the Progressive Era blurred the line between patients' choice to hasten death and society's perceived need to improve the genetic composition of the human population. The survival of the right to die movement depended on collective action to reclaim and redefine the idea of merciful death for the terminally ill through public awareness, information dissemination as well as policy advocacy. As pluralism contends, the organic process in which aid in dying groups have emerged, spun off, renamed themselves, and merged have all been, at least in part, a function of the policy environment and the interest shared by the organizations' leadership. Still, as economic/transcational theorists would argue, shared interests alone cannot sustain an organization. By identifying its niche constitutuency and a benefit that could induce membership early in its existance, Hemlock's resources and membership fueled a national death with dignity movement. Finally, as the neo-pluralist perspective posits, the extent to which an organization can influence policy will always depend on factors within the policy environment. ESA certainly could not control the damage done to the right to die movement in the United States by public sentiment against eugenics because of World War II; nor was Hemlock prepared for the effect co-founder Wickett's suicide would have on Washington State's first initiative campaign in 1991.

Aid in dying interest groups' most critical contribution to the movement has always been education. Remarkably, even as individual members of ESA demonstrated a stronger allegiance to eugenics than aid in dying, their steadfast commitment to hastening death as an organization sustained the movement during and after World War II when the public shunned anything associated with the word "euthanasia." Pope Pius XII's support for the refusal of life-sustaining treatment enabled the ESA to broaden the scope of right to die policies by serving as an information resource that would promote other legalistic transactional approaches to advance planning including, most recently, Physician Orders for Life-Sustaining Treatment (POLST). It was also SRD, a later incarnation of ESA, that revived the aid in dying debate in the late 1970s, which set the stage for the Hemlock Society and the next generation of interest groups to play a pivotal role in making and, in recent years, protecting death with dignity laws in the courts.

Still, as this chapter demonstrates, a comprehensive discussion about the relevant actors and groups and their ongoing effort for reform must also include the courts as a policymaking institution. The next chapter traces the judicial branch's participation according to its repeated involvement in making determinations about a patients' voluntariness and competence and as the final arbitors of the constitution, to ultimately decide whether a fundamental right exists to choose death.

NOTES

1. A collaboration between the Dr. Haiselden and a Hearst journalist resulted in the 1916 motion picture film entitled *The Black Stork*, which was based on the Bollinger case. The film remained in theatres until 1928 (Dowbiggin 2003).

2. Valery Garrett estimates approximately 73 percent of the founders were also members of eugenics groups. Garrett. 1998. "The Last Civil Right? Euthanasia Policy and Politics in the United States, 1938–1991." PhD dissertation, University of Santa Barbara.

3. Walker's (*Mobilizing Interest Groups in America: Patrons, Professional, and Social Movements* [Michigan: University of Michigan, 1991]) adaptation of selective benefits, which originated from (Mancur Olson, *The Logic of Collective Action: Public Goods and the Theory of Groups*, Harvard Economic Studies (Cambridge,

MA: Harvard University Press, 1965) ; James Q. Wilson, *Political Organizations* (New York, New York: Basic Books, 1974).) includes informational (e.g., publications, research, conferences), material (travel packages, insurance, discounts on consumer goods), solidary (friendship, networking opportunities, and purposive (advocacy, governmental representation, and involvement in public affairs).

4. Dickinson served as ESA president from 1946 until his death in 1950. Jones became executive vice president in 1942 and remained until her death in 1965 (Dowbiggin 2003).

5. *State of Connecticut v. Carol Paight* (1950) (unreported).

6. The bill it proposed to the Connecticut legislature, "Proposed Bill: A Suggested Solution to the Problem of Relief for Those Incurable Sufferers Who Desire Euthanasia" lacked guidance on who would administer the drug as well as which patients could petition for it (Dowbiggin 2003).

7. "40 cc of Air." *Time*, January 9, 1950, p. 13.

8. Pope Pius XII, "The Prolongation of Life: An Address of Pope Pius XII to an International Congress of Anesthesiologists." in *Death, Dying and Euthanasia*, Horan, Dennis J. and David Mall, eds. (University Publications of America: Washington, 1977), 281–92. As Dowbiggin (2007) explains, the announcement served two purposes. First, flexibility on this policy area might weaken criticism of the Church's opposition to birth control and premarital sex. Second, publicly supporting palliative care might give the Church added strength in opposing aid in dying policies.

9. Taylor, a former director of the American Birth Control League of America, served as president from 1962 to 1964.

10. McKinney, whose term began in 1965, was ESA's last president.

11. Fletcher, a moral theologian and author of the 1954 best seller and foundation for the bio ethics discipline, *Medicine and Morals: The Moral Problems of the Patient's Right to Know the Truth; Contraception; Artificial Insemination; Sterilization; Euthanasia,* is recognized as one of the most influential people the right to die movement (Dowbiggin 2003; Fletcher 1954).

12. Moore (1887–1972) was the cofounder of the Population Crisis Committee in Washington and the inventor of the Dixie Cup. Interest in aid in dying at the end of his life, stemmed, in part, from his support of the population control movement which peaked in the United States in the 1960s and 1970s. Specifically, Fletcher supported abortion and voluntary sterilization as the only means for controlling it (Dowbiggin 2003).

13. Joseph Fletcher and the other aid in dying activist members of SRD unsuccessfully tried to block the merger through litigation. Fletcher died in 1991.

14. In 1995, Robert Wood Johnson Foundation started Last Acts, a national communications campaign comprised of 800 national health and consumer groups interested in improving end of life care. L. De Milto, "Assessment of Last Acts Program Provides Recommendations for Future Direction." *Robert Wood Johnson Foundation*, October 1, 2002, https://www.rwjf.org/en/library/research/2002/10/assessment-of-last-acts-r--program-provides-recommendations-for-.html.

15. Based on the summary from Partnership for Caring (PFC), "Partnership for Caring (PFC): America's Voices for the Dying," http://www.partnershipforcaring.

org/HomePage/.in OCLC WorldCat and Google Books that only provides the book title.

16. The British police investigated Humphry, who admitted his own role but refused to name the physician who prescribed the drugs. Humphry was never formally charged (Dowbiggin 2007; Euthanasia Research & Guidance Organization (ERGO), "About Derek Humphry," 2018 (2010), www.finalexit.org/about_derek_humphry.html#career.

17. Anne Fadiman, "Death News: Requiem for the Hemlock Quarterly," *Harpers* 288, no. 1727 (April 1994): 75–80, 82.

18. Mero had become an advocate for PAD after losing his father to a long-term illness and a brother-in-law to AIDS.

19. Humphry was never accused of direct involvement in Wickett's death. However, suspicion his separation and divorce from her in 1989 led him to resign as Hemlock's executive director in 1992 (Dowbiggin 2003). Humphry's legislative pursuits continued with a new right-to-die organization, the Euthanasia Research and Guidance Organization (Patients Rights Council, "Assisted Suicide & Death with Dignity: Past, Present & Future—Part I," 2017 (2005), http://www.patientsrightscouncil.org/site/rpt2005-part1/.

20. ORS 127.800-995.

21. 546 US 243 (2006). See Ball (2017) for a more detailed explanation of the case and the Court's decision.

22. Before his 1999 conviction for second-degree murder and the illegal delivery of a controlled substance associated with the death of his last patient, Thomas Youk, the State of Michigan made repeated attempts to thwart Kevorkian's activities by prosecuting him four times, suspending his medical license, and passing laws that first explicitly outlawed assisted suicide (1992) and then made participation a felony (1998). Kevorkian was sentenced to twenty-five years but released in eight years for good behavior, after which he continued to speak publicly for PAD until his death in 2011. Biography.com, "Jack Kevorkian Biography." *A&E Television Networks*, December 3, 2015, https://www.biography.com/people/jack-kevorkian-9364141.

23. The organization was named in memory of Jack Kevorkian's nineteenth assisted suicide, Merian Frederick (Right to LIfe of Michigan, "Proposal B—Ballot Proposal on Assisted Suicide," Right to LIfe of Michigan, https://www.rtl.org/prolife_issues/propb_1998.html.

24. According to the Pro-Life Infonet, Citizens for Compassionate Care combined several state interest groups including Right to Life Michigan, the Michigan Disability Rights Coalition and the Michigan State Medical Society. The Pro-Life Infonet, "Michigan Assisted Suicide Supporters Launch." *Women and Children First*, n.d., http://www.euthanasia.com/mada.html.

25. Citizen's for Compassion Care spokesperson, Tom Ferrell, told the *Detroit Metro Times* that the organization spent $5.3 million on attack TV ads against Proposal B. December 16, 1998. "Killing Assisted Suicide," *Detroit Metro Times*, December 16, 1998, https://www.metrotimes.com/detroit/killing-assisted-suicide/Content?oid=2188416.

26. According to Right to Life Michigan, then Michigan State Democratic Senator Gary Peters, who introduced Michigan's third aid-in-dying bill, S.B. 653 in 1997, was an honorary co-chairman of the proposal. HB 4134, sponsored by Democratic Representative Lynne Martinez (D-69) and SB 0640, sponsored by Democratic Senator Jim Berryman (D-16), were introduced in 1995. Both bills died in committee.

27. In 1996, Barbara Coombs Lee replaced Ralph Mero as the executive director of CID. In addition to leadership changes (long-time Hemlock member Faye Girsh became executive director), Hemlock also launched the Caring Friends program in 1996 to mirror death assistance services provided by Ralph Mero's Compassion in Dying. To improve the organization's public appeal and shed Humphry's uneven reputation, in 2003, the board hired a nonprofit executive to run the organization with Girsh as Senior Vice President. Hemlock Society became End of Life (EOL) Choices. A year later the name would change again when it united with CID as Compassion and Choices. In the fall of 2004, members angered by the merger established Final Exit Network to offer suicide assistance to individuals who are not terminally ill and to research ways to "self-deliver" (Patients Rights Council, "Assisted Suicide & Death with Dignity: Past, Present & Future—Part I".).

28. Robert Orfali, *Death with Dignity: The Case for Legalizing Physician-Assisted Dying and*
Euthanasia. Minneapolis, MN: Mill City Press, 2011.

29. The National Hemlock Society, state chapters, Oregon Right to Die, and Oregon's governor financially supported and actively campaigned for the referendum. Opposition included Maine Citizens against the Danger of Physician Assisted Suicide and the Coalition for Compassionate Care of the Dying. Patient's Rights Council. 2000. "Maine Targeted to Promote National Right-to-Die Agenda." *Patient's Rights Council* 14, no. 2 (2000).

30. Since 1995, nine death with dignity bills have been defeated in the Massachusetts legislature: H 3173 (1995), H 1543 (1997), H 1543 (1997), H 1468 (2009), H 2233 (2011), H 3884, H 1998, H 1991 (2015), SD 744 (2017) and HD 950 (2017).

31. Marcia Angell, "No Choice but to Die Alone," *The Washington Post*, February 24, 2002, https://www.washingtonpost.com/archive/opinions/2002/02/24/no-choice-but-to-die-alone/e685dd88-45ba-4418-8414-0d8dd59f664c/?utm_term=.dad9a768abf8.

32. Ballotpedia,"Massachusetts 'Death with Dignity' Initiative, Question 2 (2012)." *Ballotpedia*, n.d., https://ballotpedia.org/Massachusetts_%22Death_with_Dignity%22_Initiative,_Question_2_(2012).

33. Carey Goldberg, "Why Mass. 'Death with Dignity' Ballot Initiative Isn't Back This Year." *WBUR*, July 7, 2016, http://www.wbur.org/commonhealth/2016/07/07/assisted-suicide-mass.

34. CID was organized as a 501 (c)(3) organization.

35. 505 US 833 (1992); 850 F. Supp.1454, 1467 (W.D. Wash. 1994).

36. *Compassion in Dying v. State of Washington*, 62 F. 3d 299, 299 (9th Cir. 1995). *Compassion in Dying v. State of Washington*, 79 F.3d 790, 798, 838 (9th Cir. 1996).

37. The three-judge panel *Quill v. Vacco*, (80 F. 3d 716, 718 (2d Cir. 1996) upheld the lower court's due process but sided with the plaintiff's equal protection argument.

38. 117 S. Ct. 2258, 2275.

39. "Medically Assisted Suicide" (H.0470) in 1993, and "An Act Relating to Rights of Terminally Ill Patients" in 1995 (H.0335), 1997 (H.0109), and 1999 (H.0493), which would have allowed terminally ill patients to receive aid in dying within a year of death instead of the standard six months. With virtually no media attention or legislative interest, all the bills died in committee.

40. Dick's father, who suffered a severe stroke and Ginny's cousin, who eventually died of cancer wanted aid in dying but could not receive it in Vermont.

41. During the 2005–2006 legislative session, Bill 168**,** the Vermont Death with Dignity Act, was introduced by Representatives Malcolm Severance (R-Chittenden 7-1), William Aswad (D-Chittenden-3-1), and David Zuckerman (D-Chittenden-10) but failed to get out of committee. Zuckerman, Aswad, and several others sponsored H.44/S.63 "Patient Choice and Control at End of Life," in 2007, which made it out of committee but lost on the floor, 82 to 63. The 2009 bill (H.455/S.144) also stalled. The measure returned 2011/2012 legislative session as H.274/S.103 but neither bill advanced.

42. In his farewell address in 2016, Shumlin spoke about his father, George Shumlin, who at the age of eighty-eight, relied on aid in dying in 2014 to end his suffering from cancer of the esophagus. "In my wildest dreams when I signed that bill, I never thought that my own dad, who was suffering from a miserable terminal cancer, would be able to die with dignity in his own state, so thank you." Mollie Reilly, "Vermont Governor Says His Dying Father Used State's Death-With-Dignity Law." *Huffington Post*, January 5, 2017, https://www.huffingtonpost.com/entry/peter-shumlin-father-death-with-dignity_us_586ebbbfe4b099cdb0fc53fa.

43. Compassion & Choices, "Volunteer Spotlight: Dick and Ginny Walters." *Compassion and Choices*, July 9, 2015, https://compassionandchoices.org/news/volunteer-spotlight-dick-ginny-walters/.

44. The Associated Press, "Leader behind Vermont's Aid-in-Dying Law Uses It, Ends Life." *NBC News*, October 16, 2015, https://www.nbcnews.com/news/us-news/leader-behind-vermonts-aid-in-dying-law-uses-it-ends-n446296.

Chapter 4

The Courts

State laws that explicitly criminalize aid in dying date back to 1828.[1] Today, 45 states in the country had such laws. Even though criminal law throughout the United States dictates that a charge of murder requires intent (as opposed to motive) as a mental state and a condition for conviction, for much of the first half of the twentieth century, those involved in the death of terminally ill people could generally expect leniency within the criminal justice system. Even in cases without clear evidence that the victims/patients wanted to end their lives, prosecutors were often unwilling to exercise their discretionary authority to charge them. When *mercy killing* cases did go forward, rarely did jurors find defendants guilty, and if they were, judges tended to opt for lenient sentences. As Lavi's research shows, half of the 70 *mercy killing* cases documented in the United States between 1920 and 1970 were never tried in court. Of the remaining 33 cases with available court results, 22 were acquitted, and only a handful were convicted of murder (145).

The Darwinian themes embodied in the eugenics movement's distortion of aid in dying also pervaded defense attorneys' arguments and judges' rulings, suggesting that leniency reflects prosecutors, jurors, and judges subscribing to the larger theoretical framework that supported forced sterilization by the state and viewed aid in dying of incurables as a key component to the furtherance of society. Legal protections for victims were secondary to protections for participants in their death and to the economic and biological good of removing unproductive members from society.

A transformation in the doctor-patient relationship during the latter half of the century called for a redefinition of the role of doctors at the end of life in the law and among the medical community. Today's patient-centered approach stems from a socio-legal and medico-legal culture that protects patients' right to self-determination to express an interest in ending life, or when their preferences have not been documented, the courts can determine when it is in their best interest to discontinue life-sustaining treatment. As the people who diagnose, evaluate, treat, and makes recommendations about patients' condition, physicians undoubtedly play a critical role in end of life care decision making. Both the law and the medical community began to put society's interest in the sanctity of life and patients' preferences at the end of life ahead of doctors' duty to save lives. The US Supreme Court has confirmed that when it is the patient's expressed will, physicians can let death occur by withholding or withdrawing treatment. Initiating death is another matter. Today, while there are seven jurisdictions that explicitly permit aid in dying, five states—Nevada, North Carolina, Utah, West Virginia, and Wyoming—still do not legally prohibit aid in dying statutorily or by common law.

As aid in dying activists and interest groups have sought to expand patient's rights to hasten inevitable, imminant death, both supporters and opponents have called on federal and state courts to determine the constitutionality of the laws prohibiting and sanctioning physician aid in dying as well as to establish a constitutional right to aid in dying. Where the courts have obliged, they have generally upheld PAD state laws. However, the belief in the sanctity of life is so deeply embedded in the constitutional history of the United States, to date, no state high court nor the US Supreme Court has established PAD as a fundamental right of terminally ill patients. The Montana Supreme Court decision in *Baxter v. Montana* allowed for PAD because there were neither legal precedents nor statutes that precluded it, but the opinion stopped short of finding an affirmative constitutional obligation to permit it and provided no parameters to implement PAD.

The expansion of patient's rights at the end of life in the United States reflects the complex interplay between the legal system and society's interpretation of legal and ethical behavior. A law and society approach provides a framework to investigate the three major questions state and federal courts have been asked to address regarding the right to die: 1) Is aid in dying a crime?; 2) Where are the lines between terminating or withdraw life-sustaining treatment for competent and incompetent patients?; 3) Do terminally ill patients have a fundamental right to hasten their deaths?

MERCY KILLING OR MURDER?

In considering guilt or innocence, jurors considered a variety of factors including the defendant's relationship to the victime. *Mercy killings* cases typically involved persons close to the victim—spouses, parents, and children. In *People v. Roberts*, for example, Frank Roberts was found guilty of first degree murder for aiding in the death of his wife, Katie, who was terminally ill with multiple sclerosis, by providing her a poisonous drink.[2] He confessed and was sentenced to life in prison, but appealed the court's decision. Although Michigan did have a law sanctioning suicide, which precluded him from prosecution as an accessory to Katie's suicide, there was a statute that treated administering poison as first-degree murder. The Michigan Supreme Court confirmed his sentence. By contrast, when Harry C. Johnson was charged with murder after asphyxiating his cancer-stricken wife in 1938 in Nassau County, New York, a psychiatrist testified before the grand jury that saying Johnson was "temporarily insane," so and they did not bring an indictment.[3]

Jurors would also consider the finality of the victim's diagnosis before death and the extent to which defendants were involved in providing care. In 1950, a Detroit Symphony musician Eugene Braunsdorf placed his twenty-nine-year-old daughter, Virginia, described as a "spastic incapable of speech," in a private sanitorium. Fearful about care after his death, he took her from the sanitarium, stopped his car, put a pillow behind her head, and shot her five times. He then attempted to end his own life by shooting himself in the chest twice. He was found not guilty by reason of temporary insanity.[4] Three years later, a father in Phoenix, Arizona by the name of Herman Nagle committed a similar crime. Fourteen years after his wife's death, the former retired New York police officer and sole caretaker of his twenty-eight-year-old daughter who suffered from cerebral palsy was diagnosed with cancer. Concerns about her care following his death led him to shoot and kill her while she slept in her wheel chair. In an interview conducted from his jail cell, he told the reporter that he had been motivated by love, and that he felt her declining health and constant pain made his act justifiable. "It was a terrible thing to do," he said "Don't think I regard it lightly."[5] He was charged with first-degree murder but was acquitted on the ground of temporary insanity after twenty minutes of jury deliberation.[6]

Two factors explain the infrequency of guilty verdicts prior to the patients' rights era. First, investigations are difficult if the family or other witnesses are unwilling to cooperate, and these cases often involved family members. Second, juries and judges' consideration of motive as a mental state has often prevented convictions. At common law, intent has always been a requirement of criminal liability. Motive, on the other hand, has never been a recognized defense but is a factor in sentencing determinations. The courts' lenience suggests that sentimentality (motive) often superseded the judge's instructions and the evidence resulting in jury nullification or recommendations for mercy in sentencing.

As access to health care improved over the course of later half of the twentieth century and health insurance became more accessible, courts' leniency toward *non-physician* defendants decreased significantly.[7] Still, judges and juries in *mercy killing* cases involving physicians remained sympathetic, or, at least, reluctant to convict and impose punishment. There was often a problem of causation. Without witnesses to the act or an admission by the physician, the court has to make a direct, causal linkage between the physician's behavior and the patient's death. It was often difficult to separate hastening death from medical treatment. Table 4.1 reports the seventeen physicians in the United States who have been indicted for murder, apart from a case I will treat separately, that of Dr. Jack Kevorkian. All were acquitted, had charges against them dismissed, had their guilty verdicts overturned, or were convicted but served no prison time, except for one who committed suicide before trial.

Jack Kevorkian is the only doctor who served significant prison time for aiding people in ending their lives. The former pathologist who labeled himself as a "death consultant" but was called "Doctor Death" by the press, participated in 130 deaths with the aid of two patient-operated machines he invented—"Thanatron" (Greek for "instrument of death") and the "Mercitron" ("mercy machine")—from the back of his converted 1968 Volkswagon van.[8] Kevorkian's willingness to help strangers end their lives regardless of their mental competence or whether terminal diagnosis was present drew the ire of the medical community and detracted from the goals of the right to die movement. Of the sixty-nine deaths Kevorkian participated in between 1990 and 1998, only seventeen involved terminally ill persons.

Kevorkian's engagement in mercy killing was atypical for several reasons. First, assisting in hastening death made him a celebrity, which was uncommon among those accused of PAD. Far surpassing the fame that Dr. Harry J. Haiselden's obtained for his repeated acts of infanticide in the 1910s, Kevorkian remains one of the most recognizable names in the modern PAD debate.[9] He has been the subject of numerous books, scholarly articles, news reports, and TV show segments. He appeared on the *Phil Donahue* show in 1990 and was the subject of a 2010 HBO movie, *You Don't Know Jack.*[10]

Perhaps due to the level of fame Kevorkian obtained, legislative and civil liberties discourse and action followed the media attention to his actions. As Kevorkian's acts garnered headlines during the 1990s, New York and his home state of Michigan convened commissions to consider legalization. The nation's first PAD ballot initiative campaign, Initiative 119, was launched in Washington State in 1991 and the right to die movement realized its first legislative victory in 1997 when Oregon enacted the Death with Dignity Act. However, the debate also seemed to precipitate greater restrictions in some states. The US Supreme Court dealt the movement another blow in 1997 when it upheld the constitutionality of state laws that ban PAD in *Vacco v. Quill* and *Washington v. Glucksberg.*[11] Moreover, at least eight states enacted laws that condemned or strengthened their aid in dying laws.[12]

Table 4.1 U.S. Physicians Indicted for Murder in *Mercy Killing* Cases

Year	*Defendant*	*Location*	*Summary*
1925	Dr. Harold Blazer	Montevista, CO	Dr. Blazer was indicted and tried for the murder of his daughter, Hazel, who had cerebral spinal meningitis and was described as having a mind of a baby and limbs of a 5-year-old. Blazer, his wife, and another daughter had cared for Hazel for 30 years. Months after his wife's death, Blazer placed a chloroform soaked handkerchief over her face until she died. He was acquitted because the jury could not arrive at a verdict[1]
1950	Dr. Herman S. Sander	NH	Dr. Sander injected 40 cc. of air into the vein of cancer patient, Mrs. Abbie Borroto, causing her death. Unaware that his actions constituted a crime, Sander noted his act in her hospital record. When the county medical referee told him he had committed murder, Sander allegedly replied that the law should be changed but later stated his notes had been "casual dictation" meant to "close out the chart." At the end of the three-week trial and 70 minutes of deliberations, the jury returned a verdict of not guilty (Baughman and Bruha 1973, 52) *New Hampshire v. Sander* (1950) (unreported case).
1972	Dr. Vincent Montemarano	Nassau County, NY	Dr. Vincent Montemarano, a chief surgical resident at the Nassau County Medical Center in New York, was tried for the willful murder of a patient. Dr. Montemarano injected his 59-year old, throat cancer patient, Eugene Bauer, who had days to live, a fatal dose of potassium chloride which killed him five minutes later. Jurors deliberated for 55 minutes. Montemarano was found not guilty.[2]
1982	Dr. Robert J. Nejdl & Dr. Neil L. Barber	Los Angeles County, CA	Drs. Nejdl and Barber were tried for murder for terminating life support from 55-year-old Clarence Herbert, at the request of the patient's family. Mr. Herbert had suffered a heart attack that left him brain dead three days after intestinal surgery in 1981. He died six days after the doctors disconnected tubes keeping him alive. In 1983, an appeals court dismissed the charges against the doctors.[3]
1985	Dr. John Kraai	Fairport, NY	Dr. John Kraai was charged with the murder of his friend, 81-year-old friend Frederick Wagner, who suffered from Alzheimer's disease and gangrene. During a visit at his nursing him, Kraai injected Wagner with a fatal dose of Demerol (insulin). Fearful of conviction, 76-year-old Kraai took his own life with Demerol while free on bail three weeks later.[4]

(*Continued*)

Table 4.1 (Continued)

Year	*Defendant*	*Location*	*Summary*
1986	Dr. Joseph Hassman	Berlin, NJ	In 1986, Dr. Joseph Hassman pled guilty for injecting his mother-in-law, Ester Davis, who suffered from Alzheimer's disease and was confined to a nursing home, with Demerol (insulin) through her feeding tube. A New Jersey Superior Court sentenced Hassman to probation for two years, imposed a $10,000, and ordered him to perform 400 hours of community service.[5]
1987	Dr. Peter Rosier	Fort Myers, FL	Patricia Rosier was terminally ill with cancer and she attempted suicide with sleeping pills, but failed. Her husband Dr. Rosier gave her a fatal dose of morphine. In 1988, Dr. Rosier was charged with the murder but a Pinellas County, Florida Circuit Court jury acquitted him.[6]
1989	Dr. Donald Caraccio	Troy, MI	Dr. Caraccio was charged with first-degree murder for injecting 74-year-old Juliette Cherry-Sapp, who suffered from gangrene, heart disease, and kidney failure, with a lethal dosage of potassium chloride in 1988. After accepting Caraccio's guilty plea to poisoning with intent to kill, the judge sentenced him to five years of probation with community service.[7]
1990	Dr. Richard Schaeffer	Redondo Beach, CA	Dr. Schaeffer and Mary Seifert were arrested on suspicion of killing Seifert's ailing 75-year-old husband, Melvin, by lethal injection. There were released during the investigation and the charges against both were dismissed one year later (Humphry 2005).
1992	Dr. Marilyn Dargis	Michigan City, IN	Dr. Dargis, an emergency room doctor, was indicted by a Michigan City grand jury in 1992 for reckless homicide for inappropriate use of morphine and suffocation of 66-year-old Albert O'Neil, who had suffered a heart attack. After repeated unsuccessful attempts by Dargis and paramedics to resuscitate him, Dargis injected morphine into O'Neil's corpse so his wife would not see his last "agonal" breaths. Dargis entered a plea agreement to perform 300 hours of community service in indigent medical care in LaPorte County and had to submit to a monthly or quarterly psychiatric report for three years in return for a suspension of the charges against her (Alpers 1998).[8]

1994	Dr. Eva Carrizales	Riverdale, GA	Neonatalist Dr. Carrizales was charged with the death of 39-day-old terminally ill Omar Jiminez. When the infant suffered kidney failure, Dr. Carrizales withdrew life-sustaining treatment without parental consent. After 20 hours of deliberation, the judge declared a mistrial after the jury remained hopelessly deadlocked, 7–5. The district attorney dismissed the charges and the Georgia Composite Board of State Medical Examiners decided not to impose sanctions (Alpers 1998).[9]
1997	Dr. Ernesto Pinzon-Reyes	Highlands County, FL	Dr. Pinzon-Reyes was tried for first-degree murder of 70-year-old Rosario Gurrieri, who was terminally ill with cancer of the lung, liver, and spine. In October 1996, Pinzon-Reyes injected Gurrieri with a lethal combination of morphine, Valium, and potassium chloride, causing his death less than an hour later. Pinzon-Reyes was acquitted of murder but found guilty of lying in the patient's charge to conceal his act. The Florida State Board of Medicine suspended his license for two years, with credit for times served and a stay for the remainder of the sentence (Alpers 1998; Kollas et al. 2008).[10]
1998	Dr. Stan Naramore	St. Francis, KS	Dr. Naramore was charged with murder and attempted murder of two terminally ill patients in 1992. Suspecting brain death, Dr. Naramore withdrew life-sustaining treatment from 81-year-old Chris Willt, who had suffered a stroke and required medical ventilation. His death took place eight minutes later. Dr. Naramore was also accused of attempting to hasten death for 78-year old Ruth Leach, who suffered from metastatic cancer, by administering a deadly dose of morphine. The doctor's actions were not directed by the patients or their families in either case. Naramore was convicted on both counts and sentenced to concurrent terms of 5 to 20 years in July 1998. A year later, Kansas Court of Appeals reversed the jury's conviction and acquitted Naramore.[11]
1998	Dr. C. Douglas Wood	Muskogee, OK	Dr. Wood was indicted for first-degree murder of 86-year-old Veterans Affairs Hospital patient, Virgil Dykes, in 1994. Wood injected Dykes, who suffered from tuberculosis, emphysema, congestive heart failure, and septic stomach ulcer, with 20 mL of potassium chloride, which caused his death minute later. In 1998, a jury convicted Wood of the lesser offense, involuntary manslaughter. He was sentenced to five months in prison and fined $5,000. In 2000, the 10th US Circuit Court of Appeals agreed 3–0 to overturn the involuntary conviction with the option to retry him for the same charge.[12]

(Continued)

Table 4.1 (Continued)

Year	*Defendant*	*Location*	*Summary*
1999	Dr. Robert A. Weitzel	Layton, UT	In 1996, after receiving permission from the patients' families, Dr. Weitzel, a board-certified psychiatrist, began implementing a palliative approach to five patients housed in a geriatric psychiatric ward at Davis Hospital and Medical Center in Layton, using opioid analgesics to manage pain and dyspnea. In 1999, the Utah Department of Commerce revoked Weitzel's controlled substance license, suspended his medical license, and filed five murder charges against him. A jury found Weitzel guilty of two counts of negligent homicide and sentenced him to 1 to 15 years in prison in July 2000. The following month, the Utah Coalition to Improve End of Life Care reviewed Weitzel's case and although the coalition found no criminal wrongdoing, they were advised to withhold his finding from Weitzel's attorney. Weitzel filed a motion for a new trial, which was granted in January 2001. In 2002, a new jury acquitted Weitzel on all counts (Kollas et al. 2008).[13]
2007	Dr. Anna Pou	New Orleans, LA	Dr. Anna Pou and nurses Cheri Landry and Lori Budo were arrested and charged with the second-degree murder of at least 17 patients at New Orleans Memorial Medical Center during Hurricane Katrina. Confronted with concerns about raising floodwater, the loss of electricity and air conditioning, Pou, Landry, and Budo had used lethal doses of morphine and the sedative midazolam by injection without permission of the patients or their families. Almost two years later, a New Orleans grand jury declined to indict.[14]
2010	Dr. Lawrence Egbert Jr.	Atlanta, GA	Retired Baltimore anesthesiologist and then-medical director of the Final Exit Network (FEN), Dr. Egbert, along with FEN former president, Ted Goodwin, group member Claire Blehn, and regional coordinator Nicholas Alec Sheridan, were indicted on charges of racketeering, assisting a suicide, and tampering with evidence that led to the death of 58-year-old John Celmer, who suffered deep depression after surviving oral cancer. Prosecutors were forced to drop the charges against the four after the Georgia Supreme Court agreed that the state's anti-assisted suicide law violates the First Amendment.[15] In 2012, Republican Georgia Governor Nathan Death signed Bill HB 1114, a comprehensive prohibition of assisted suicide.[16]

2011	Maricopa County, AZ	Dr. Egbert, along with three FEN volunteers, Wye Hale-Rowe, Roberta Massey, and Frank Lansner, were indicted in Georgia for conspiracy to commit manslaughter of 58-year-old Jana Van Voorhis, who was not terminally ill at the time of her death but suffered from mental health issues and depression. According to the police report, she believed she had holes in her belly, feet, and liver, and that someone had attempted to poison her with pesticides. Voorhis was found dead in her home April 2007 after she placed a plastic helium-attached hood over her head (which FEN calls an "exit hood"). Langners and Hale-Rowe were accused of showing Voorhis how to use the hood while Egbert and Massey's involvement related to processing applications through the organization to receive assistance to hasten her death. After a three-week trial, Arizona jury acquitted all four defendants of the manslaughter.[17]
2012	Apple Valley, MN	57-year-old Doreen Nan (Gunderson) Dunn, who suffered from intense chronic pain after a medical procedure and depression, used a FEN Exit Guide to end her life by asphyxiation with the use of an "exit hood" on May 30, 2007. In March 2012, Dr. Egbert—then, case coordinator Robert Massey—exit guides Ted Goodwin, and then FEN president, Jerry Dincin, along with FEN as a corporate entity, were charged individually on 17 counts, which included assisting in a suicide and gross misdemeanors for interfering with a death scene. Following a 90-minute deliberation, FEN was convicted of interfering with a death scene and ordered to pay $33,000 in fines and restitution. Dincin, who was also present the day Dunn died, died in 2013. Egbert was granted immunity for his testimony two weeks before the trial began. In 2017, the US Supreme Court declined to hear the case.[18]

(Continued)

[1] International News Service, "Favors Execution of Idiots," *The Houston Chronicle*, November 8, 1925, p. 2.

[2] Roy Silver, "Nurse Says She Saw Montemarano Give Patient Fatal Enjection." *New York Times*, January 24, 1974.

[3] *Barber v. Superior Court*, 147 Cal. App. 3d 1006.

[4] Bruce Hilton, "As Funds For Elderly Dry Up, Mercy Killings Rise," *Chicago Tribune*, January 25, 1987, http://articles.chicagotribune.com/1987-01-25/features/8701070113_1_mercy-killing-mercy-or-murder-roswell-gilbert (June 9, 2018).

[5] *People v. Hassman* (unreported), *New York Times*, December 20, 1986.

[6] *People v. Rosier* (unreported), "Doctor Freed in Wife's Death," *New York Times*, December 2, 1988.

[7] Joe Swickard, "Doctor Given Probation for Mercy Killing," *Detroit Free Press*, April 5, 1989.

[8] Northwest Indiana Times, "News in Brief," *The Times*, July 30, 1993; Richard D. Walton, *The Indianapolis Star*, February 26, 1993.

[9] Steve Glasser, "Mistrial in Georgia Doctor Murder Trial, *United Press International*, November 4, 1994.

[10] Barbara Fowler, "Doctor's Acquittal Act of Compassion." *Orlando Sentinel*, July 6, 1997, http://articles.orlandosentinel.com/1997-07-06/news/9707030547_1_pinzon-father-died-brother-and-i.

[11] *State v. Naramore*, 965 P.2d 211 (Kan. Ct. App. 1998).

[12] Robert E. Boczkiewicz, "VA Doctor's Conviction Overturned," *NewsOK, March 30, 2000,* https://newsok.com/article/2691804/va-doctors-conviction-overturned.; *United States v. Wood*, 207 F.3d 1222 (10th Cir. 2000).

[13] Weitzel was tried for the murders of the following victims: Ellen B. Anderson, 91, who died December 30, 1995; Judith V. Larsen, 93, who died January 3, 1996; Mary R. Crane, 72, who died January 3, 1996, and Lyndia M. Smith, 90, who died January 8, 1996, and Amy Joi Bryson and Jim Rayburn Deseret, who died September 23, 1999. Weitzel, who was indicted at the time of his arrest, pled guilty to two counts of federal prescription fraud for writing prescriptions for his own personal use and was sentenced to one year and a day in prison in August 2001 and served his time after the 2002 retrial. Amy Joi Bryson and Jim Rayburn, "Doctor Charged with Murder: 5 Charges Filed in Deaths of Elderly Patients, *Deseret New*, September 23, 1999, http://www.deseretnews.com/article/719282/Doctor-charged-with-murder.html; The National Registry of Exonerations, "Robert Weitzel," *Newkirk Center for Science & Society*, n.d., https://www.law.umich.edu/special/exoneration/Pages/casedetail.aspx?caseid=4453.

[14] Sheri Fink, "The Deadly Choices at Memorial," *The New York* Times, August 25, 2009, https://www.nytimes.com/2009/08/30/magazine/30doctors.html.

[15] Sarah Childress, "The Evolution of America's Right-to-Die Movement," *PBS Frontline*, November 13, 2012, www.pbs.org/wgbh/frontline/article/the-evolution-of-americas-right-to-die-movement/.

[16] Alex Schadenberg, "The Final Exit Network and Its Leader Are Indicted for Assisted Suicide," *Euthanasia Prevention Coalition*, May 15, 2012.

[17] Sarah Kliff, "Laurence Egbert: Assisted Suicide's New Face," *Newsweek*, March 14, 2010, www.newsweek.com/lawrence-egbert-assisted-suicides-new-face-69677.

[18] Staff. "Right-to-Die Group Convicted of Assisting in Minnesota Suicide," *The Baltimore Sun*, May 14, 2015, www.baltimoresun.com/health/bs-hs-right-to-die-group-trial-20150514-story.html. Following a two-year investigation, in 2014, the Maryland Board of Physicians revoked medical license of Dr. Egbert, dubbed by the media as the "New Doctor Death," for actions deemed "unethical and illegal." He told the press that he had participated in nearly 300 deaths nationwide. He died of a heart attack on June 9, 2016 at the age of 88. Kelly, Jacques. June 17, 2016. "Dr. Lawrence D. Egbert, Physician Who Advocated Assisted Suicide, Dies," *The Baltimore Sun*, June 17, 2016, www.baltimoresun.com/news/obituaries/bs-md-ob-lawrence-egbert-20160617-story.html.

In Michigan, even as Kevorkian tried to change the law, the state government became increasingly punitive in their legislative attempts to stop him. In 1990, Michigan had no statute regarding aid in dying, however, Republican Governor John Engler signed SB 211 in 1993, which established a commission to study aid in dying in Michigan but also included a provision that made it a felony. Within weeks of its enactment, the American Civil Liberties Union filed a lawsuit on behalf of Michigan cancer patients and health professionals challenging the constitutionality of the newly enacted law. Later that year, Judge Richard Kaufman finds a constitutional right to "rational" suicide thus striking down SB 211. The Michigan Court of Appeals stuck down the law on technical grounds but the Michigan Supreme Court upheld the law and ruled that the act of providing aid in dying is a common law felony. The US Supreme Court refused to hear Kevorkian's appeal. As the legality of Michigan's law traveled through the state appellate courts in 1994, Kevorkian stood trial for the murder of his seventeenth patient, thirty-year-old Thomas Hyde, who had Lou Gehrig's disease. Kevorkian's defense concentrated on a loophole in the law that permitted pain relief. Specifically, he argued that the carbon monoxide he provided that was only meant to relieve his pain as opposed to end Hyde's live. The juror agreed and acquitted him. He also attempted to put a constitutional amendment for aid in dying on the statewide ballot that same year but failed to get necessary number of signatures on the petition. His defense contended again in 1996 that his intent was to relieve the pain of seventy-two-year-old Merian Frederick, who had Lou Gehrig's disease, and sixty-one-year-old bone cancer patient Dr. Ali Kalili in 1993, and not to cause their deaths. The loophole defense led to another acquittal. In 1998, a Kevorkian-inspired grassroots interest group called Merian's Friends proposed a measure that would have legalized physician aid in dying. Proposal B was defeated by a resounding margin of 71 percent to 29 percent. The same year, Governor Engler signed SB 200 making aid in dying a felony punishable by a maximum of five years in prison or a $10,000 fine. The loophole in Kevorkian's previous acquittal was closed and he was convicted the following year.

Kevorkian's unprecedented public candor about his willingness to assist in suicide led to only one conviction.[13] A Michigan County judge enjoined him from offering aid in dying in 1990, and the state Board of Medicine of Michigan revoked his license to practice medicine in Michigan the next year. Still, between 1990 and 1999, prosecutors tried Dr. Kevorkian for murder five times. Three of the cases ended in acquittal and the fourth ended in a mistrial. The final indictment came three days after CBS's *60 Minutes* aired a segment entitled "Death by Doctor" showing Kevorkian administering a lethal injection to fifty-two-year-old Thomas Youk, who suffered from Lou Gehrig's Disease, in 1998. Kevorkian was charged with murder in the first degree, assistance in suicide, and delivery of a controlled substance in Youk's death.

Kevorkian represented himself in trial. He was sentenced to between ten to twenty-five years in prison. In 2001, the appeals court rejected his appeal.[14] He was released in 2007 after serving eight years, in part because he was terminally ill with Hepatitis C. Kevorkian died in 2011. For all of the attention Kevorkian received, aid in dying was not the only end of life matters to capture headlines and forge new judicial paths.

THE RIGHT TO REFUSE AND WITHDRAW LIFE-SUSTAINING TREATMENT

The patient autonomy movement emerged against the backdrop of the social movements of the 1960s and 1970s. The women's movement's denouncement of medical paternalism and advocacy of women in taking a more active role in their health care significantly impacted the role of organized medicine in death and dying. Increasingly, patients were unwilling to see doctors as unquestionable sources of wisdom, and this supported a feeling that more medicine might not result in better health. The public's esteem for physicians had declined. Many saw hospitals as the site of lonely, painful deaths, and technology designed to sustain life was perceived as prolonging needless suffering. After decades of unsuccessful attempts to legalize aid in dying and the Catholic Church's acceptance of refusal of treatment in the late 1950s, the notion of privacy emerged as the focus of the modern right to die movement and the crux of the constitutional basis for establishing refusal rights for medical treatment *In re Quinlan and Cruzan v. Director, Missouri Department of Health.*

The growing number of requests the Euthanasia Society of America received for living wills signaled the increasing sense of the importance of documenting treatment preferences. The legal battle with hospital administrators that the parents of twenty-one-year-old Karen Quinlan waged in 1975 to discontinue life support, not only gave the nation a front-row seat to the right to die issue but was also the catalyst for the rapid adoption and diffusion of living will statutes across states during the 1970s and 1980s. After ingesting a combination of alcohol and prescription drugs caused Quinlan to collapse, stop breathing, and fall into a coma, EMTs saved her life, but a loss of oxygen to her brain left it severely damaged. She was diagnosed as in a persistent vegetative state with no hope of recovering consciousness. Her parents, both devout Catholics, sought guardianship to remove artificial life support. When her primary care physician and the hospital refused because she was not brain dead, the Quinlans filed a court petition. A lower New Jersey court rejected the petition. Recognizing the importance of the matter, the case bypassed the intermediate court and was granted certiorari by the New Jersey Supreme Court in 1976. Citing the constitutional right to privacy found in *Griswold v. Connecticut* and confirmed in *Roe v. Wade*, the court recognized, for the first time, a patient's right to privacy as providing the right to decline life-sustaining treatment in certain situations. It was also a first for what would become known as the "Substitute Judgment Test" establishing the rights of incompetent individuals to discontinue life support through a court appointed guardian.[15] The hospital was ordered to remove the respirator.[16] That same year, California became the first state to enact a living will law. By 1990, 41 states and the District of Columbia passed living will legislation.

The *Quinlan* opinion established a right to refuse life-sustaining treatment in New Jersey, but the US Supreme Court would have to hear a case involving an incompetent patient without an advance directive for a similar right to exist in other states. After roughly a decade and half of deference to the states on the right to die controversy, the Supreme Court issued its first opinion in *Cruzan v. Director, Missouri Department of Health* during its 1989 term. The petitioners—the parents of Nancy Beth Cruzan—had waged a nearly eight-year legal battle to remove the gastrointestinal tube that provided food and water to their twenty-five-year-old daughter who entered a persistent vegetative state after an automobile accident. While she did not have a living will, Cruzan had expressed a wish not to remain alive unless she could live "at least halfway normally." The Cruzans requested the hospital remove her feeding tube. It refused, citing a Missouri law that required "clear and convincing" evidence that the patient desired removal. The Cruzans sued the hospital and the state's Department of Health. A lower court found that a letter to her friend about her preferences was sufficient and she had a fundamental right to refuse the feeding tube. The Missouri Supreme Court reversed the decision, arguing that "no person can assume that choice for an incompetent in the absence of the formalities required under Missouri's Living Will statutes or the clear and convincing inherently reliable evidence absent here." The US Supreme Court affirmed the decision of the Missouri Supreme Court by a vote of 5 to 4 on the grounds that the letter was insufficient to establish the patient's desire. Nevertheless, recognized a constitutional right for competent individuals to refuse medical therapy, including advanced technological care and feeding tubes, grounded in the Fourteenth Amendment. Five weeks after the ruling, with three new testimonies from the patient's friends affirming she would want to end her life in her current condition, the Cruzans asked a Missouri probate judge for a hearing. Judge Charles Teel found the evidence credible. The State Attorney General's Office declined to appeal Teel's decision, and Cruzan died shortly after the tube was removed.

THE ONGOING FIGHT FOR A RIGHT TO DIE

The Supreme Court's 1990 decision in *Cruzan* solidified the federal government's position to defer to states to make determinations on any rights beyond those established for competent patients to refuse life-sustaining treatment. Since then, a patchwork quilt of legislative and judicial decisions across states addressing the two areas of law continues to shape the right to die movement, refusal rights of incompetent patients, and PAD. States took two approaches to laws addressing persistent vegetative cases. One approach was to establish the highest threshold of in civil matters, the "clear and convincing evidence" standard. The other empowers judges with discretionary power to determine the acceptability of "substituted judgement" of guardians or the outcome that is in best interest of the patient. Ultimately, without documented instructions from the patient about end of life care, each guideline, to some extent, tasks the individuals involved with the patient and society in general to make moral judgments about the appropriateness of the decision to continue or withdraw life-sustaining treatment.

The fifteen-year public saga over the life and death of Terri Schiavo that began in 1990 personified the all too common medical, ethical, legal, and familial conflicts that arise when patients do not have advance directives. Schiavo was twenty-five years old when a potassium imbalance caused her to sustain a cardiac arrest and enter a persistent vegetative state. A medical malpractice lawsuit against Schiavo's fertility specialist enabled her husband, Michael Schiavo, to afford both experimental and rehabilitative therapy for many years.[17] During this time, he became her guardian and had a do not resuscitate order (DNR) put in her medical chart. Asserting that his wife would not want to remain in a vegetative state, in 1998, Michael sought to remove her feeding tube. Terri's parents, Robert and Mary Schindler, both devout Catholics, objected. Michael then filed his first petition requesting the removal of Terri's feeding tube. Since Terri did not have a living will, Florida law would require "clear and convincing evidence" of her intent, just as like Missouri had in *Cruzan*. After almost two years of testimony, Pinellas Florida Circuit Republican Judge George Greer ruled in 2000 that the feeding tube should be removed. The Schindlers appealed. They also lobbied the state legislature to pass that a law that would give then Governor Jeb Bush the authority to reinstate the feeding tube. In 2003, the Florida legislature passed "Terri's Law" which granted Governor Bush the authority to issue a "stay" of any court order directing the discontinuation of life-sustaining treatment, so long as specific conditions were met.[18] After the Florida State Supreme Court unanimously struck Terri's Law down as a violation of the separation of powers mandated by the Florida Constitution, Congress tried to intervene by passing its own version of "Terri's Law" in 2005.[19]

Eager to demonstrate his pro-life beliefs, Jeb's brother, President George W. Bush eagerly returned to Washington during Easter break to sign the special emergency law that gives a Florida District Court jurisdiction to initiate a new inquiry into the legal and medical questions surrounding Schiavo's health.[20] In an opinion written by the US Circuit Court Judge Stanley Birch Jr., a conservative appointee of President George H. W. Bush, the court decided that "The legislative and executive branches of our government have acted in a manner demonstrably at odds with our Founding Fathers' blueprint for the governance of a free people—our Constitution."[21] After numerous legal challenges, the enactment of state and federal law, and the resurgence of the Catholic Church in the right to die debate, Michael prevailed when the Schindlers exhausted their appeals. Terri Schiavo died March 31, 2005.

While the Schiavo controversy facilitated a national discourse on advance directives in the 1990s, two court cases, one in Washington State and the other in New York, put the question of whether the terminally ill have a constitutional right to aid in dying before the Supreme Court. In 1994, a consortium of terminally ill patients, five doctors, and the aid in dying Hemlock Society breakout group, Compassion in Dying, filed a suit in federal district court in Seattle, Washington challenging its statute, which deemed aid in dying a class C felony punishable by imprisonment for up to five years and a fine of up to ten thousand dollars.[22] The statute was enacted in 1854, but it had rarely been enforced. While the crux of their legal argument stemmed from the Due Process Clause of the Fourteenth Amendment, each of the three groups of plaintiffs alleged violations on somewhat different grounds. The patients, sixty-nine-year-old cancer patient, "Jane Roe," forty-four-year-old AIDS patient, "John Doe," and sixty-nine-year-old emphysema sufferer, "James Doe," argued that due process and equal protection under the law affords citizens a right to PAD without governmental interference. The physicians—Harold Glucksberg, assistant professor of oncology, John P. Geyman, chair of the Department of Family Medicine at the University of Washington School of Medicine, Thomas A. Preston, chief of cardiology at the Pacific Medical Center in Seattle, Abilgail Halperin, family practitioner and clinical instructor, and Peter Shalit, also a clinical instructor and internist—relied on the Fourteenth Amendment, but asserted that the law violated physicians' rights. Even though they faced no legal threat, Compassion in Dying, which operated in the shadows of the law by offering guidance to terminally ill patients on how end their lives with the use of prescription drugs, filed the suit to preempt criminal prosecution by explaining their actions as an exercise of their constitutional right of choice in the face of imminent death.[23] The decision by Carter appointee District Judge Barbara Rothstein on May 3, 1994, ruled in favor of the plaintiffs, accepting their argument based in the Fourteenth Amendment. Rothstein reasoned that the significant difference between the liberties afforded to mentally competent individuals to refuse life-sustaining treatment and physician aid in dying implies that Washington's law constitutes a violation of the Equal Protection Clause. However, the State of Washington appealed and a divided Ninth Circuit reversed Judge Rothstein's decision.[24] In 1995, the court of appeals granted an unprecedented rehearing *en banc* that provided another reversal, 8 to 3.[25] Washington State lawyers appealed the circuit court's decision to the US Supreme Court.

In the meantime, a parallel case erupted in New York in the same period. Dr. Timothy Quill, who had become known for his *New England Journal of Medicine* article defending his involvement in hastening the death of one of his patients, was indicted in 1994 for prescribing the lethal dose of barbiturates that end the life of the forty-five-year-old female patient discussed in the article. Two other physicians, Samuel C. Klagsbrun, a Westchester psychiatrist and Howard A. Grossman, an AIDS doctor, and their terminally ill patients, Rita Barrett, who was dying of cancer, and two AIDS victims, George A. Kingsley and William A. Barth, challenged New York's law prohibiting aid in dying, also on the basis that it violated the Fourteenth Amendment's Due Process and Equal Protection Clauses.[26] Nixon appointee US District Court Judge Thomas P. Griesa of the Southern District of New York ruled in favor of the defense in 1994, but the Second Circuit review of the matter in the fall of 1995 reversed the decision rejecting the plaintiff's claim that the Due Process and Equal Protection Clauses sanctions PAD. In a 3 to 0 decision written by Reagan appointee, Judge Roger Miner, the thee-judge panel confirmed Griesa's position on due process agreeing that PAD lacks historical roots and is therefore not a "fundamental liberty" protected by the Due Process Clause. However, the panel agreed with the plaintiff's equal protection argument that the state had no legitimate interest in interfering with a doctor's prescribing a drug to a mentally competent patient.[27]

The Supreme Court heard a consolidation of the Washington and New York cases in January 1997.[28] The Court's unanimous overruling of the Circuit court's decisions and upholding the Washington and New York's laws prohibiting aid in dying was no surprise to Court observers. The Rehnquist Court typically demonstrated a reluctance to expand rights under the Due Process or Equal Protection Clauses. The death of all the respondents in the cases made it even more difficult for respondents who, based on facial challenge, had to establish that "no set of circumstances exists under which the act would be valid."[29] Had they been alive, the cases would have been heard "as applied challenging" where the attorney would have only had to demonstrate that the two statutes were invalid "as applied to the terminally ill patients." The attorneys for the respondents were arguing their cases largely before a conservative Court. The two only left-leaning justices on the Court, Ruth Bader Ginsberg and Stephen Breyer, were appointed by Democratic

President Bill Clinton. Who filed amicus briefs and, on whose behalf, further signaled resistance to policy innovation. The majority of the briefs filed in the case aligned with the mostly conservative court in opposing PAD. Of the 60 briefs filed, 41 were filed by organizations such as Not Dead Yet, the National Hospice Association, medical and nursing associations, the Catholic Church, Agudath Israel, and the US Department of Justice. The American Civil Liberties Union (ACLU), the American Medical Students Association, 36 religious organizations, and surviving family members filed briefs in support of aid in dying.

What was also telling about the Court's emphatic rejection of any constitutional right to PAD was the variation in the arguments presented in six separate concurring opinions. Even though the Court had been willing to protect rights that had not been traditionally protected, Chief Justice Rehnquist was unwilling to do so in his majority opinion in *Glucksberg* by stating that, "the history of the law's treatment of assisted suicide in this country has been and continues to be one of the rejection of nearly all efforts to permit it." He argued in majority opinion in *Vacco* that since the equal protection clause did not created any substantive rights, it had not been violated.

Stevens, Souter, O'Connor, Ginsberg, and Breyer's concurring opinions emphasized how the laws prohibiting PAD may be unconstitutional as applied. Still, none of the Justices argued that PAD is a fundamental right. Stevens agreed with the majority opinion's history and tradition claim but pointed out that Washington had authorized the death penalty which challenges the claim that the preservation of the sanctity of life outweighs a dying patient's dignity and alleviating suffering. Even though most of Justice Souter's concurrence addressed technical issues regarding the Due Process Clause, he too signaled support of aid in dying in some circumstances in the future. Justice O'Connor challenged the scope of laws by contending having been applied to a narrower class of patient; the laws may have been unconstitutional. As a breast cancer survivor herself, O'Connor also understood the frequency in which families must face decisions about hastening death for themselves or a terminally ill family member which, at some point, states would need to address. Justice Ginsberg's concurring opinion explained her agreement with Justice O'Connor's reasoning. It is Breyer's opinion though that addresses the semantics problem with PAD by challenging the Court's characterization of the claimed liberty interest as a "right to commit suicide with another's assistance" by instead using the term death with dignity which means having "personal control over the manner of death, medical assistance, and the avoidance of severe physical suffering." He argued that a law that prevents terminally ill patients access to pain medication at the end of life would be unlawful. Over all, as Sunstein contends, the 1996 ruling neither established a fundamental right for PAD nor precluded states from forging their separate legal paths on the issue. Instead, it showed deference to the states while keeping an option open for future Supreme Court rulings that might curtail state power.

CHALLENGING BANS ON PAD IN THE STATES, 1997–2015

In the years following *Glucksberg* and *Vacco,* right to die activists brought suits in five states, only to be disappointed in the highest courts of Florida (1997), Alaska (2001), Michigan (2001), Connecticut (2010), and New York (2017). A New Mexico court judge briefly established a fundamental right to PAD in 2014 but the decision was overturned by the New Mexico Court of Appeals in 2015 and confirmed by its supreme court a year later. *Baxter v. Montana* (2009) states that the state Constitution does not prohibit aid in dying and refers the issue to the state legislature, which has failed repeatedly to pass any laws to permit, ban, or regulate aid in dying.

The plaintiffs in *Baxter v. Montana* included four physicians—oncologist, hospice co-founder and founder of the local chapter of Physicians for Social Responsibility, Dr. Stephen Speckart, Clinical Associate Professor of Medicine at the University of Washington, Dr. C. Paul Loehnen, former nursing home medical director, Dr. Lar Autio, and University of Montana School of Pharmacy clinical faculty member, Dr. George Risi Jr.—joined Robert Baxter, a seventy-five-year-old truck driver who had terminal lymphocytic leukemia, and PAD advocacy organization Compassion & Choices.[30] Their petition argues that Montana's statutes that criminalized PAD violated Article II, Declaration of Rights, Sections 3 (inalienable rights), 4 (individual dignity), and 10 (right to privacy) of the Montana Constitution. Within hours of Baxter's death on December 5, 2008, First District Judicial Court of Lewis and Clark County Judge Dorothy McCarter issued a summary judgement in favor of the plaintiffs, stating that that "constitutional rights of individual privacy and human dignity, taken together, encompass the right of a competent terminally-ill patient to die with dignity." In a 5 to 2 decision, the state supreme court affirmed the decision on December 31, 2009, but only on statutory grounds.[31] Drawing upon Montana's 1985 Rights of the Terminally Ill Act that recognizes patient autonomy in end of life medical care decisions and protects physicians from prosecution when following their wishes, the court concluded that although the state constitution does not guarantee a right to receive aid in dying, the court determined that "nothing in state supreme court precedents or Montana statutes specifies that PAD is against public policy."[32] So the Montana Supreme Court allows PAD but it would be the responsibility of the legislature to specify the provisions and regulations.

But legislating PAD in Montana remains at a partisan standstill to date. Death with dignity appeared on the states' legislative agenda for the first time in 2011. Democratic Senator Anders Blewett introduced Senate Bill 167, which would have created a framework for PAD, and Republican Senator Greg Hinkle introduced Senate Bill 116 that sought to prohibit PAD. Neither bill passed. In 2013, a Republican, House of Representatives Member Krayton Kerns introduced House Bill 505 to prohibit PAD, and a Democrat, Senator Dick Barrett introduced Senate Bill 220 that would have mirrored Oregon's Death with Dignity law, but, once again, the bills did not pass. In 2015, Republican House Member Gerald (Jerry) Bernnett introduced "The Physician Imprisonment Act" (HB 477) that sought to imprison physicians for up to ten years for PAD. Dick Barrett introduced a pro-PAD bill (Senate Bill 202).[33] Neither bill was successful. To challenge the state supreme court's decision as well as to criminalize PAD, in 2017, Republican Representative Brad Tschida sponsored a bill that states that "physician aid in dying is against public policy, and a person's consent to physician aid in dying is not a defense to a charge of homicide against the aid in dying physician" (HB 536). The bill passed the Montana State House on a second reading 52 to 48, but the final vote failed in a 50–50 tie.[34]

Four years after the Robert Baxter's death, in 2012, a New Mexico resident who had just received an advanced uterine cancer diagnosis set about to find out, as she told a reporter, "what I needed to do if I would like to perhaps have a more peaceful and gentle death." The only patient named in the case Aja Riggs joined a case with the American Civil Liberties Union of New Mexico and Compassion & Choices filed on behalf of New Mexico oncologists, Dr. Katherine Morris and Dr. Aroop Mangalik who sought to exempt PAD from the existing aid in dying law. On January 13, 2014, New Mexico's Second Judicial Court Judge Nan Nash issued a permanent injunction prohibiting the criminalization of aid in dying and thus establishing a fundamental constitutional right to receive and provide PAD under the substantive Due Process Clause of the state's constitution.[35] However, Gary King, New Mexico's attorney general, filed an appeal with the encouragement of the New Mexico Archdiocese and pro-life groups two months later.[36] The appeal was successful. In nearly a 150-page opinion, a 2 to 1 vote decision by the three-judge New Mexico Court of Appeals reversed the decision in August 2015, stating that the New Mexico Constitution does not provide a fundamental right to PAD.[37] The fracture between the lower and appellate court gave the ACLU and Compassion & Choices a compelling argument to file an expedited emergency petition to the New Mexico Supreme Court. The writ was granted but the outcome sent a stunning blow to the right to die movement. In June 2016, the New Mexico Supreme Court upheld the Court of Appeals decision, unanimously, upholding the state's prohibition of PAD in New Mexico.

PAD advocates turned their attention to the New Mexico legislature. In January 2017, Democrat House members Deborah Armstrong and Bill McCamley and Senators Elizabeth Stefanics introduced the "End of Life Options Act" in their respective chambers.[38] House Bill 171 deviates from previous laws and proposals by loosening standard safeguards such as permitting non-physicians (e.g., advance practice nurse, physician assistant) to diagnose a patient and prescribe lethal drugs, broadening the definition of "terminal illness," and eliminating the waiting period in between diagnosis and prescription request and the requirement for a second opinion by a consulting health care provider, among other provisions. The bill passed the House Health and Human Services Committee 4 to 3, along party lines, and was referred to the House Judiciary Committee where action has been postponed indefinitely. An amended Senate version (SB 252) made it through Senate Public Affairs and Senate Judiciary Committee approval but the full Senate voted it down, 20 to 22.[39]

CONCLUSION

The first century of end of life jurisprudence which begin roughly in the 1920s reflects society's steadily evolving values about death and dying. It has been over twenty years since *Glucksburg* and the future for PAD as a fundamental right both nationally and subnationally remains uncertain. As of 2015, legislation exists in forty states that criminalize aid in dying. Yet, as the repeated acquittals of doctors who have administered life-ending treatment demonstrate, with or without statutory, common law, or even constitutional rights, societal interest in and tolerance for hastening death remains. *Quinlan* and *Cruzan* solidified a right to privacy that includes refusal and withdrawal of medical treatment including food and hydration when competent adults have made clear expressions about preferences such as advance directives. The cases also represented a painfully obvious truth about advance directives—few Americans have them. Despite the well-intentioned efforts over the last fifty years by legislatures, courts, administrative agencies, and professional associations to promote the use of advance directives, research shows that only about a third of US adults complete a living will, health care power of attorney, or both.

When patients' medical choices at the end of life are unknown and they are unable to communicate them, their family members, the medical community, and society at large have looked to the courts to make determinations about and establish parameters for withdrawing treatment for incapacitated persons. In one of several decisions the Supreme Court would make on the issue of a right to die demonstrating its deference to state policymakers, *Cruzan* enabled states to decide whether it wanted to apply Missouri's higher standard of clear and convincing evidence for surrogate decision making. While several states including New York, Michigan, and Texas use this standard, Florida's application of the standard in the Terri Schiavo case put the national spotlight on the complexities in determining whose evidence is more "clear and convincing" (e.g., spouse, parents) and the amount of information needed to meet it. The Schindlers presumed that their daughter would have chosen to remain in persistent vegetative state for the remainder of her life. Her spouse disagreed. Multiple Florida courts agreed with him. The sufficiency of the evidence as to Schiavo's wishes and the outcome of the case will remain a matter of legal and political debate.

There is also the matter of locating a constitutional right to PAD within the federal or a state constitution. While the Supreme Court's decisions in *Glucksberg* and *Vacco* failed to strike down state laws prohibiting PAD, they also did not legally prevent states from permitting it. While activists have found success through state legislatures and direct democracy, the right to die movement has yet to convince a state supreme court that a constitutional right exists for PAD. Legislative efforts to adopt PAD in Montana remains stalled. As status quo persists in some states and a flurry of legislative and judicial activity in others, the push and pull between law and society continues.

As the public and increasingly partisan reform battle continues to play out in statehouses and courthouses across the country, since the early 1990s, health care professionals across states have chosen to work together to solve a major flaws in advance health care directives—protecting patent's preferences at the end of life. The next chapter reviews the history of advance directives, to trace the emergence of the Physician Orders for Life-Sustaining Treatment (POLST) Paradigm as a policy innovation designed and implemented by health care coalitions.

NOTES

1. Act of December 10, 1828, ch. 20, § 4, 1828 N.Y. Laws 19.
2. *People v. Roberts*, 211 Mich. 187, 178 N.W.2d. 690, 694 (1920), overruled in *People v. Campbell*, 335 N.W.2d 27 (Mich. App. 1983). In *People v. Kevorkian*, 447 Mich. 436, 527. W.2d 714 (1994) the Michigan Supreme Court decided that the extent to which a defendant participates in death determines murder. Supplying poison would be considered passive participation and not murder. In 1998, Republican Governor John Engler signed SB 200 banning physician aid in dying.
3. *New York Times*, October 12, 1938. At 30, col. 4; *People v. Montemarano* (1974).
4. "Murder or Mercy?" *Time,* June 5, 1950.
5. "Father Killed for Love," *The Argus*, September 8, 1953.

6. *New York Times*, December 24, 1953, at 20, col. 7.

7. Silvia Sara Canetto and Janet D. Hollenshead, "Older Women and Mercy Killing," *OMEGA-Journal of Death and Dying* 42, no. 1 (2001): 83–89.

8. Thanatron administered successive doses of saline solution, a painkiller, and fatal dose of potassium chloride that would stop the heart through an IV drip. Mercitron used carbon monoxide, stored in the rear of the van, to hasten death. Andrew Tarantola. June 3, 2011. "Jack Kevorkian's Assisted Suicide Tools (and Van)" *Gixmodo*, June 3, 2011, https://gixmodo.com/5808444/jack-kevorkians-assisted-suicide-tools-and-van.

9. See chapter 3 for a compete summary of the Dr. Haiselden and the Bollinger case.

10. Adam Mazer, *You Don't Know Jack*, directed by Barry Levinson, HBO Films, 2010,

11. 521 US 793 (1997); 521 US 702 (1997).

12. Massachusetts General Laws, Chapter 201D 12 (enacted 1990); Minnesota Statute 609.215 (amended in 1992); Tennessee Code Ann. 39-13-216 (felony) (enacted 1993); Maryland Code Ann. Health Gen 5-611 (revised 1994); Louisiana Rev. State. Ann. 14:32.12 (enacted 1995); Alabama Code 1975 22-8A-10 (enacted 1981, amended 1997); South Carolina Code 1976 16-3-1090(B)(felony) (enacted 1998); and Michigan Compiled Law Ann. 752.1027 (felony) (enacted 1992); Virginia Code 8.01-622.1 (enacted 1998).

13. *People v. Kevorkian*, 248 Mich. App. 373, 639 N.W.2d 291 (2001), appeal denied; *People v. Kevorkian*, 205 Mich. App. 180, 517 N.W.2d 293 (1994), vacated & remanded; 447 Mich. 436, 527 N.W.2d 714 (1994), certiorari denied; *Kevorkian v. Michigan*, 514 US 1083 (1995); *People ex rel. Oakland County Prosecuting Att'y v. Kevorkian*, 534 N.W.2d 172, 210 Mich. App. 601 (1995), affirming injunction against Dr. Kevorkian assisting in hastening death, 549 N.W.2d 566 (Mich.), appeal denied; *Kevorkian v. Michigan*, 519 US 928 (1996), certiorari denied.

14. *People v. Kevorkian*, 248 Mich. App. 373, 639 N.W.2d 291 (2001), affirming second-degree murder conviction; *People v. Kevorkian*, 642 N.W.2d 681 (April 9, 2002), certiorari denied; *Kevorkian v. Michigan*, 537 US 881 (2002), certiorari denied; Jennifer Latson, "Why 'Dr. Death' Wanted to be Charged with Murder;" *Time*, March 26, 2015, www.time.com/3748245/Kevorkian-trial-history/.

15. Quoting *In re Carson*, 545, 241 N.Y.S.2d 288, 289 (Sup. Ct. 1962).

16. Because she was able to breath on her own and nutrition and hydration continued, Karen lived in a persistent vegetative state for another nine years, eventually die of pneumonia in 1985.

17. *In Re Theresa Marie (Terri) Schiavo* 90-2908GD-003 (Fla. Cir. Ct., Pinellas Co, February 11, 2000); 90-2908GB-003 (Fla. Cir. Ct., Pinellas Co, November 22, 2002).

18. 2003 Fla. Laws, ch. 418.

19. *Bush v. Schiavo*, 885 So. 2d at 324.

20. A Bill for the Relieve of the Family of Theresa Marie Schiavo. P.L. 109-3 (2005).

21. *Schiavo ex rel. Schindler v. Schiavo*, 404 F.3d 1270, 1271 (11th Cir. 2005).

22. The Washington Natural Death Act. Wash Rev. Code § 9A.36.060(1) (1988).
23. *Compassion in Dying v. Washington*, 850 F. Supp. 1454 (W.D. Wash 1994).
24. *Compassion in Dying v. Washington*, 49 F.3d 586 (9th Cir. 1995).
25. *Compassion in Dying v. Washington,* 62 F.3d 299 (9th Cir. 1995).
26. All three patients died of natural causes before trial. James C. McKinley Jr., "Court Urged to End Ban on Help with Suicide," *New York Times*, September 2, 1995, https://www.nytimes.com/1995/09/02/nyregion/court-urged-to-end-ban-on-help-with-suicide.html. *Quill v. Koppell*, 870 F. Supp. 78 (S.D.N.Y.1994)
27. *Quill v. Vacco*, 80 F.3d 716, 718 (2d Cir. 1996). Dennis C. Vacco had replaced G. Oliver Koppel as Attorney General of New York, and therefore the name of the case changed.
28. *Washington v. Glucksberg*, 117 S. Ct. 2302 (1996); *Vacco v. Quill*, 117 S. Ct. 2293 (1996).
29. *US v. Salerno*, 481 US 739 (1987).
30. Sean T. Murphy, "The Case of the Disappearing Plaintiffs: Robert Baxter et al vs. State of Montana." *Conscience Laws*, August 3, 2009, www.conscience.laws.org/background/procedures/assist006.aspx.
31. The case garnered amicus brief participation from interest groups on both sides of the issue. The American Medical Woman's Association, American Medical Student's Association, human rights groups, clergy legal scholars, and 31 Montana state legislators were just of the few of the groups supporting Baxter's constitutional claim. Opposition briefs were filed by the Alliance Defense fund on behalf of the Family Research Council, Americans United for Life, the American Association of Pro-Life Obstetricians and Gynecologists, and the Catholic Medical Association. The Montana Medical Association issued a statement opposing PAD but did not file a brief on appeal. Kieran Bellville, *Dying to Kill: A Christian Perspective on Euthanasia and Assisted Suicide* (Cambridge, OH: Christian Publishing House, 2014).
32. Montana Code 50-9-101-206.
33. Compassion & Choices. "Senate Committee Rejects Bill to Imprison Doctors Who Practice Aid in Dying." *Compassion in Dying*, March 2015, https://www.compassionandchoices.org/2015/03/; Patients Rights Council, "Montana," *Patients Rights Council*, n.d., www.patientsrightscouncil.org/site/montana/.
34. According to Ballotpedia, in 2017, The Republican Party controlled the Montana House, 59 to 41. Death with Dignity. 2018. "Montana." *Death with Dignity*, n.d., https://www.deathwithdignity.org/states/montana/.
35. *Morris v. Brendanburg*, WL 10672986, *6 (2d Jud. D. Ct. Bernalillo County, N.M. 2014)
36. Just as they had in *Baxter*, the American Medical Women's Association, the American Medical Student Association supported the plaintiffs, filing a joint amicus brief supporting PAD with the New Mexico Public Health Association.

The New Mexico Psychological Association and the New Mexico Chapter of the ALS Association also filed briefs in support while the New Mexico Roman Catholic Archdiocese and the Christian Medical and Dental Associations joined five New Mexico Senators and six members of House in an amicus brief in support of the State. Disability rights groups including the American Association of People with Disabilities, ADAPT, Not Dead Yet, the Autistic Self Advocacy Network, the Disability Rights Education and Defense Fund, the National Council on Independent Living, and the United Spinal Association also filed briefs on behalf of the state.

37. *Morris v. Brendanburg*, 356 P.3d 564 (N.M. Ct. App. 2015)

38. Death with Dignity, "New Mexico," *Death with Dignity*, n.d., https://www.deathwithdignity.org/states/new-mexico/.

39. There are currently 26 Democrats and 16 Republicans in the New Mexico Senate. New Mexico Legislature, "Political Composition" *New Mexico Legislature,* n.d., https://www.nmlegis.gov/Members/Political_Composition.

Chapter 5

Health Care Coalitions

In 1990, the Hemlock Society revived aid in dying advocacy in the United States by introducing a death with dignity bill in the Oregon legislature and by filing Initiative 119 in Washington. Jack Kevorkian assisted in the death of Janet Atkins, a fifty-four-year-old woman diagnosed with Alzheimer's disease, which led to his first murder charge. That same year the Supreme Court announced its decision in *Cruzan*, Terri Schiavo went into a persistent vegetative state, and Congress enacted the Patient Self-Determination Act to require medical facilities that receive federal funds to recognize advance directives and protect a patient's right to refuse life-sustaining treatment[1] As one of the most prolific decades for the right to die movement began to gain momentum, a coalition of health care professionals in Oregon sought to enhance the effectiveness of advance directives for patients nearing death. The legal transactional mode of advance planning produced a series of patient-generated legal documents that specified procedural requirements and limitations but provided few assurances that they would protect patients from needless and unwanted medical care at the end of life.

In 1990, volunteers from EMS, medicine, nursing, and long-term care professions gathered at the Center for Ethics in Heath Care at Oregon Health and Science University (OHSU). Their objective was to discuss how to bridge the fragmented health care system to honor patient's wishes as expressed in advance directives. Under the leadership of Dr. Patrick Dunn, senior scholar at the Center for Ethics in Health Care, the newly formed Oregon POLST Task Force did more than create a form; they shifted the paradigm. Their communication-centered approach does not abandon advance directives (e.g., living will, power of attorney, health care proxy, do-not-resuscitate order), but it complements them by promoting ongoing discussion between doctor and patient as well as among treating health professionals to make them more effective and reflective of the patient's preferences at the end of life. The POLST form was so named to underscore its authority as a medical order rather than, like an advance directive, a patient-directed document. The POLST Paradigm is a clinical process specifically designed for patients who have advanced chronic progressive illness, who are not expected to live a year, or who want to define their treatment preferences with a set of portable medical orders that communicate their treatment goals and preferences, bridging the communication gap between patients and the implementation of care.

To help their policy innovation proliferate, the Oregon POLST Task Force departs from the status quo mode of policy decision making through elected and appointed officials by promoting policy making through health care coalitions. The policy diffusion literature commonly attributes the spread of ideas as a process the stems from incremental policy learning by elected or appointed officials in state government. Broadly defined as alliances formed by solution-oriented key stakeholders such as patients, their families, and healthcare practitioners, health care coalitions emerged in the late 1970s and early 1980s as employer-only initiatives that emphasized health care cost containment but increasingly became a powerful tool for addressing patient-related issues such health care planning.[2] Instead of seeking regulations that would force health care professionals to use POLST, the Task Force believed that they would have buy-in if the protocol reflected the input of stakeholders working to serve the needs of both patients and practitioners. By 2002, the majority of Oregon medical facilities had implemented POLST and Wisconsin (1997), Washington (2000), Pennsylvania (2000), West Virginia (2002), and Utah (2002) had formed intrastate coalitions to pilot POLST programs. Today, POLST Paradigm programs exist in all 50 states and Washington, DC.

Although POLST has received far less media and scholarly attention than death with dignity, its predecessors, advance directives, have sought to protect patient choice at the end of life by directing or delegating end health care decisions since the 1960s with the living will.

As living will laws proliferated and other legal transactional approaches followed, a growing body of research had revealed the limitations of advance directives. Research revealed that the legal language in the advance directives often discouraged patients, who didn't understand them, from completing them. Those that would, often admitted that they didn't understand what they had signed. Because advance directives require updating as patients' goals and preferences change over time, fulfillment delays were not uncommon. Studies also show that as many as 65 to 76 percent of physicians are completely unaware that their patients have an advance directive.[3] While a 1991 Gallup poll found that 75 percent of Americans approved of living wills, only about 20 percent of adults completed them. Further, fewer than 15 percent of patients received input from their physician when developing their advance directive. Practitioners were frustrated with the current method of protecting patients' end of life preferences and sought an alternative to the status quo.

Despite the influence that health care professionals have over pain and death issues, collectively, they had left end of life policymaking to legislators, interest groups, and voters. POLST is a clinical protocol that functions as clinician-led advocacy groups designed to protect and promote patient autonomy. This chapter begins with the approach that preceded POLST, providing a historical review of documents that reflect the legal transactional approach—living wills, durable power of attorney, and do not resuscitate (DNR) orders. It explains and how their shortcomings led to POLST. As the policy innovation spread throughout the country, national organizational leadership would be necessary to provide policy guidance to developing programs and conduct ongoing research. This chapter also explains the origin and the National POLST Paradigm Initiative Task Force (NPPTF) and its underlying principle of making POLST a standard of care. State regulations and statutes and political climate have created significant variation in the implementation of POLST across states. The last section of this chapter explores the various stages of program development based on intrastate forces.

THE EVOLUTION OF ADVANCE CARE PLANNING POLICY

Medical technological advances in death and dying complicated interactions between physicians and patients. Over the course of twentieth century, Americans transitioned to dying in hospitals so that they would have access to such technology. Physicians are taught to preserve life, which sometimes brought them into conflict with patients and their families, who wanted the choice to avoid needles and unwanted life-sustaining treatment. Chicago human rights lawyer Luis Kutner responded to this problem by introducing the living will to the Euthanasia Society of American in 1967. Building from a common law and constitutional framework, Kutner described living wills as a tool that would enable individuals to set forth the terms of their health care preferences regarding the withholding or withdrawing of life-sustaining interventions in advance of any future mental or physical incapacities. The form was short, simple, and without legal force but could still be used to influence the physician or family decision making as well as protect clinicians from potential liability.

The adoption and diffusion of living will legislation with California's adoption of the Natural Death Act in 1976 addressed the legal authority issue but its shortcomings were quickly apparent. Most states only permitted the withdrawal of medical treatment from patients expected to die soon, thus excluding patients in persistent vegetative states and those suffering long decline due to Alzheimer's. They also could not anticipate future diagnoses or medical treatments available. Over-specificity left doctors, hospital administrators, and families scrambling to interpret the point at which the patient no longer felt able to make decisions or perceived certain treatments as extraordinary. When such discrepancies arose, a person holding durable power of attorney for the patient could make health care decisions on behalf of the incapacitated. Historically used in matters involving estate planning, powers of attorney existed under common law but were revoked when the principal became incompetent or incapacitated. In 1954, Virginia became the first state to permit the holder of the "durable" power of attorney to act on behalf of the principal even after the principal lost capacity. Other states adopted similar laws shortly thereafter.[4] In 1983, the President's Commission for the Study of Ethical Problems in Medicine and Biomedical and Behavioral Research promoted the use of advance directives for health decision making but questioned whether sufficient safeguards existed in the current legislation to protect against abuse. To address the issue, states either enacted special durable powers of attorney for health care statutes or added proxy provisions to living will statutes. After Pennsylvania enacted the first durable power of attorney for health care (DPAHC) legislation in 1983, DPAHC reached complete adoption in all fifty states and the District of Columbia by 1997. By itself, the durable power of attorney for health care document designated a person to act as the principal's healthcare proxy who can make health care decisions, but when executed along with a living will, it can also specify medical treatment preferences to the proxy.

DPAHCs presented patients with another legal option to express their preferences but, just like living wills, they offered no guarantee of the execution of those preferences, for three reasons. First, some states only allowed DPAHC to take effect for patients that were terminally ill or in a persistent vegetative state. Second, DPAHC relies on the agent to both understand the principal's preference and to execute it. These documents cannot control the feelings of the agent or map out all aspects of the principal's future health condition. A meta-analysis of sixteen studies of whether DPAHC assures decision making in keeping with patients found that patient-designated and next-of-kin surrogates had an overall rate accuracy of 68 percent of correctly stating the patients' medical care preferences in specific scenarios. Although based on hypothetical situations, the results suggest that the comprehension and literacy issues that often deter the usage and completion of advance directives also affect the efficacy of DPAHC.

The do not resuscitate (DNR) order was the next entry in the growing list of legalistic transactional approaches designed to help patients avoid prolonged, poor-quality lives. Cardiopulmonary resuscitation (CPR) by closed-chest message had developed in the early 1960s and soon became the standard emergency procedure perform on patients in cardiac arrest. Research found that the survival rate of all patients who had undergone CPR following hospital discharge in the United States was only 10 to 15 percent. The diminishing benefit of calling a "code blue" to perform CPR on every patient in cardiac arrest encouraged hospitals to create variations haphazardly in the level of resuscitation attempts. Since code status decisions were not standardized across health care facilities, communication among staff about a patients' DNR orders varied between purple stickers in the medical record, cryptic notes in the patient's chart, and verbal orders from shift to shift. None of these processes included methods to document the patient's preferences. The American Medical Association was the first professional organization to call for uniformity in DNR order designations in 1974. This encouraged the adoption of DNR policies across hospitals that also began to include patients and their family members in the decision making process but their participation was not mandatory and even patients that had them might be revived due to an incident at home or at a hospice care facility and they did not cover EMTs' response in those environments. In 1998, media attention to a New York hospital that still used the purple sticker designation in patient's records resulted in the enactment of the first statute governing the use of out-of-the hospital DNR orders. The legislation required signatures from both the patient (or the surrogate, in some states) and his or her doctor to execute a DNR order and required EMTs to follow them if presented with a patient's DNR form or if the patient is wearing a specifically designed identification bracelet. Before the close of the twentieth century, forty-two states had similar protocols in place, mostly through legislation.

Advance directives provided a mechanism for patients to specify a variety of details about their end of life treatment and designate a surrogate to make health care decisions on their behalf, but despite earnest intentions, a growing body of research began to show that they did not significantly reduce the number of patients receiving unwanted medical treatment. Advance directives not only requires knowledge and understanding about illnesses and treatments but also assumes that the decisions made will not change. For example, if patients knew that some medical circumstances predict very low long-term survival rates for patients who receive CPR (0 to 22 percent), fewer patients may request it. Studies have also shown that medical preferences tend to change over time. In fact, depending on a patient's age and advance directive status, one-third of a patent's end of life preferences will change less than two years after expressing them in an advance directive.[5]

PROTOCOL DESIGN AND NATIONAL ORGANIZATION DEVELOPMENT

The medical community began to converge on the idea that enhancement to the legalistic transactional approach would require communication and clinical consensus. Without ongoing dialogue between patients and physicians about end of life care planning and among health professionals to ensure the execution of patient's preferences, advance directives would remain ineffective. DNR designation in patient's medical records was a start but it needed to be made available to health professionals across medical setting. Building from several guiding principles, in 1990, the Oregon POLST Task Force set out to design a new DNR or advance directive that would promote communication, collaboration, and cooperation.[6] First, the dialogue needed to be open, inclusionary and based on consensus. Second, quality improvement would be "truth seeking" and rely on ongoing critical feedback. Third, the group sought to avoid and mitigate conflicts of interest.

The evolution of the POLST reflects the Task Force's principles. The first draft, known as the Medical Treatment Coversheet (MTC), was a simplistic and efficient one-page, hot pink form designed to facilitate and document discussions of end of life care planning between patient and physician. Physicians were to document whether the patient had advance directives and to attach them to the record. Additionally, because the form would be signed by a doctor, health care professionals treated the decisions within it, including limitations on antibiotics and artificial fluids and nutrition, as medical orders. This would make their effect immediate without further interpretation, as well as portable and recognizable across medical settings and medical professionals.[7] The Task Force piloted a program using the MTC to study its uses. They also assembled educational resources and disseminated information statewide to health professionals, health care systems, and patients and their families about it. The final draft was released as POLST in 1995. The final form was two pages to accommodate for future changes and ongoing review.[8] Table 5.1 summarizes key differences between POLST and advance directives.

Since implementation of policies rarely involves policymakers, the Task Force's ongoing involvement in POLST implementation set it apart from extant legalistic transactional approaches. The Task Force embraced the idea that POLST utilization should be voluntary and driven by clinical consensus. State legislature circumvention offered two major benefits. Although regulatory changes were necessary, this approach gave the Task Force the latitude to implement the protocol as they designed it. Specifically, POLST sought changes to the Oregon Board of Medical Examiners' administrative rule to protect EMTs, first responders, and supervising physicians from criminal prosecution when complying with patients' wishes; they carved it out by referencing medical orders executed by physicians specifically. Measure 16, the Oregon Death with Dignity Act had garnered significant media and political attention during the mid-1990s. The Task Force chose to avoid legislative scrutiny or political framing by instead focusing on educating health care professionals about the protocol. The approach proved to be successful. By 2002, POLST had become a standard of care in Oregon, used in most medical settings. Research on its use in nursing homes showed that most residents across the state were completing POLST and that percentages of adherence and portability were high.[9]

Next, the Oregon Task Force sought to help other states develop similar programs. As POLST captured the interest of health care professionals in

Table 5.1 Key Differences Between POLST and Advance Directives

Characteristics		*POLST Paradigm*		*Advance Directives*
Population	→	Advanced Progressive Chronic Conditions	→	All Adults
Timeframe	→	Current Care	→	Future Care
Where Completed	→	In Medical Setting	→	In Any Setting
Resulting Product	→	Medical Orders (POLST)	→	Advance Directive
Surrogate Role	→	Can Do If Patient Lacks Capacity	→	Cannot Do
Portability	→	Provider Responsibility	→	Patient/Family Responsibility
Periodic Review	→	Provider Responsibility	→	Patient/Family Responsibility

Source: Data from table 1 of Charles P. Sabatino and Naomi Karp, "Improving Advanced Illness Care: The Evolution of State POLST Programs," *AARP Public Policy Institute*, 2011, https://assets.aarp.org/rgcenter/ppi/cons-prot/POLST-Report-04-11.pdf.

other states, ongoing and widespread ethical use of POLST would require institutional support and meaningful engagement of stakeholders. Both would be needed to reduce the potential of clinician domination over health care decisions and to avoid lawmakers perceiving POLST as an attractive money-saving measure. For POLST to become a standard of care nationwide would take decades of education to change the culture as well as a coalition of local stakeholders to remain vested in these pursuits. The Oregon Task Force decided to form a national leadership organization to aid in this process by establishing and maintaining POLST standards while also helping other states develop what became known as the POLST Paradigm. With administrative support from OHSU, Dunn's direction, and representation from health care professionals, researchers, and lawyers from the six already implementing states—Oregon, Wisconsin, West Virginia, Washington, Pennsylvania, and New York, the thirteen-member Task Force convened in 2004 to establish the National POLST Paradigm Task Force (NPPTF).[10]

The policy diffusion literature commonly attributes the spread of innovation to an incremental learning model with only a few states adopting the new policy at a time, then it gains momentum, and slows again after but half of the states in the country adopt the innovation. This process forms a bell-shaped

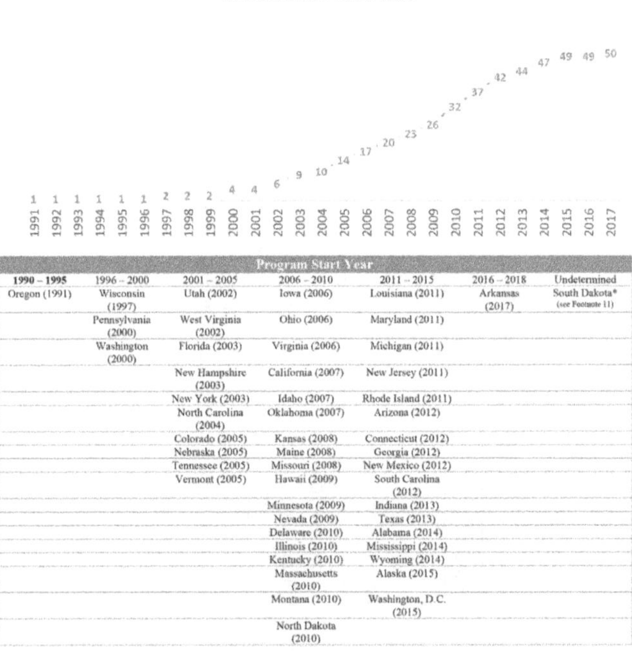

Program Start Year						
1990 – 1995	1996 – 2000	2001 – 2005	2006 – 2010	2011 – 2015	2016 – 2018	Undetermined
Oregon (1991)	Wisconsin (1997)	Utah (2002)	Iowa (2006)	Louisiana (2011)	Arkansas (2017)	South Dakota* (see Footnote 11)
	Pennsylvania (2000)	West Virginia (2002)	Ohio (2006)	Maryland (2011)		
	Washington (2000)	Florida (2003)	Virginia (2006)	Michigan (2011)		
		New Hampshire (2003)	California (2007)	New Jersey (2011)		
		New York (2003)	Idaho (2007)	Rhode Island (2011)		
		North Carolina (2004)	Oklahoma (2007)	Arizona (2012)		
		Colorado (2005)	Kansas (2008)	Connecticut (2012)		
		Nebraska (2005)	Maine (2008)	Georgia (2012)		
		Tennessee (2005)	Missouri (2008)	New Mexico (2012)		
		Vermont (2005)	Hawaii (2009)	South Carolina (2012)		
			Minnesota (2009)	Indiana (2013)		
			Nevada (2009)	Texas (2013)		
			Delaware (2010)	Alabama (2014)		
			Illinois (2010)	Mississippi (2014)		
			Kentucky (2010)	Wyoming (2014)		
			Massachusetts (2010)	Alaska (2015)		
			Montana (2010)	Washington, D.C. (2015)		
			North Dakota (2010)			

Figure 5.1 Number of POLST Paradigm Programs Established 1991–2017.
Source: "National POLST Paradigm Program Designations," National POLST Paradigm, n.d., http://polst.org/programs-in-your-state/.

curve when plotted over time and the cumulative frequency of innovation adoption over time forms an S-shaped curve. However, as figure 5.1 indicates, the diffusion of POLST was more like an upward slope as more and more states implemented it. A sudden positive feedback cycle during the mid-2000s seemed to speed adoption across states. In 2017 Arkansas became the last state to start a POLST Paradigm Program.[11] To date, twelve states have made the POLST Paradigm a part of its standard of care by utilizing the form statewide.[12] To improve the form's accessibility to health care professionals, programs in Oregon, Idaho, New York, and West Virginia have gone a step further by creating statewide registries to house POLST forms.[13]

In an effort to balance NPPTF standards with coalition autonomy, individual programs determine their scope (regional or statewide) and name (e.g., New York and Maryland use Medical Orders for Life-Sustaining Treatment, MOLST, and Indiana, Virginia, Idaho, and Tennessee use the name Physician Orders for Scope of Treatment). However, endorsement by the national organization requires local or statewide coalition leadership, participation by key stakeholders, the use of a standardized form that complies with the national program requirement, and ongoing training of health care professionals across the continuum of care in the paradigm.[14] Programs must also demonstrate evidence of consideration of its Seven Core Elements of Sustainability: (1) voluntary POLST completion; (2) patient or surrogate/proxy knowledge of the form's completion; (3) ongoing conversations about the patent's current diagnosis, prognosis, and treatment options between patient and healthcare professional; (4) limit use of the POLST Paradigm (form) to only the seriously ill, frail patients, or those who are likely to expire within a year; (5) promote ongoing dialogue between patients and their health care professionals about patients' preferences; (6) encourage patients to complete Sections A (Cardiopulmonary Resuscitation options) and B (Medical Interventions or Treatment) of the form; and (7) design forms to require the patient's or surrogate/proxy's signature.[15]

POLST PROGRAM NATIONAL LANDSCAPE

The speed with which programs in different states developed, as well as their commitment to the National POLST Paradigm, varies significantly. Figure 5.2 captures the current program designations based on an application process that evaluates scope of use in the state, stage of development, and conformity to its standards. Only three states—Oregon, California, and West Virginia—have earned the "mature program" designation, which suggests the greatest level of adoption of the paradigm.[16] The programs in these states followed the national standards and guidelines to make the POLST Paradigm a statewide standard a care for terminally ill patients nearing death. Programs designated as "endorsed" may be regional or pilot programs that are progressing toward statewide use by developing strategies for ongoing implementation, education,

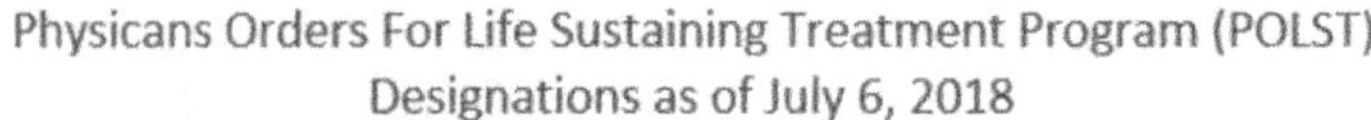

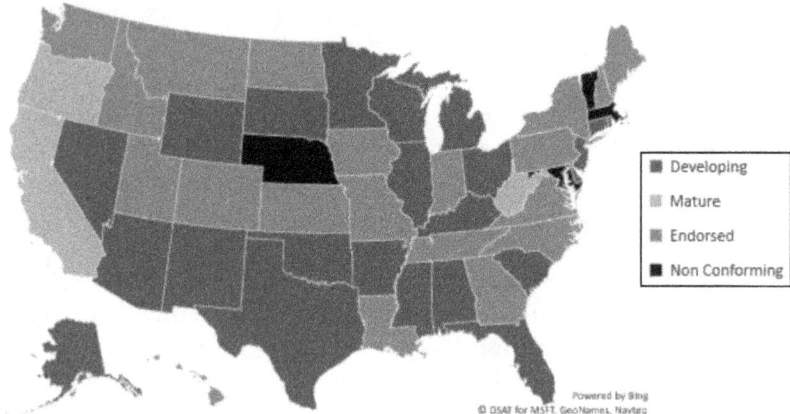

Figure 5.2 POLST Program Designations as of July 6, 2018.
Source: "National POLST Paradigm Program Designations," National POLST Paradigm, July 6, 2018, http://polst.org/programs-in-your-state/.

and quality control and by navigating and addressing legal and regulatory barriers that preclude POLST use in their state. There are twenty endorsed states. "Developing programs," of which there are twenty-four, are working on the initial design of their POLST form, active use of the POLST Paradigm as well as those working toward statewide implementation. Programs must demonstrate ongoing efforts to expanding their program to maintain the "developing" designation. Finally, the national organization designates the programs in Maryland, Massachusetts, Nebraska and Vermont as non-conforming.[17]

Depending on existing laws and regulations related to end of life decision making and care, the state's political climate, and attitudes about POLST among health care professionals and patients in the state, program implementation has occurred in four ways—adoption of state laws recognizing POLST, administrative regulation of POLST, incremental program development, or health care coalition consensus. Figure 5.3 is a graphical representation of the duration of program existence before statutory or regulatory recognition.[18] Although the level of specificity of statutes and regulations varies across states, governments were involved in the establishment of POLST Programs in fourteen states and Washington, DC.[19] While Louisiana's statute, for example, includes the actual language used in the form, Idaho's statute specifies which health care professional can sign the POLSTs but is intentally vague about the form requirements and procedures to give the POLST program more autonomy in form development and evaluation.[20] Overall, the legislative or regulatory approaches ensure form uniformity, legal clarity, and that health care providers have immunity from criminal or civil liability or disciplinary sanctions.

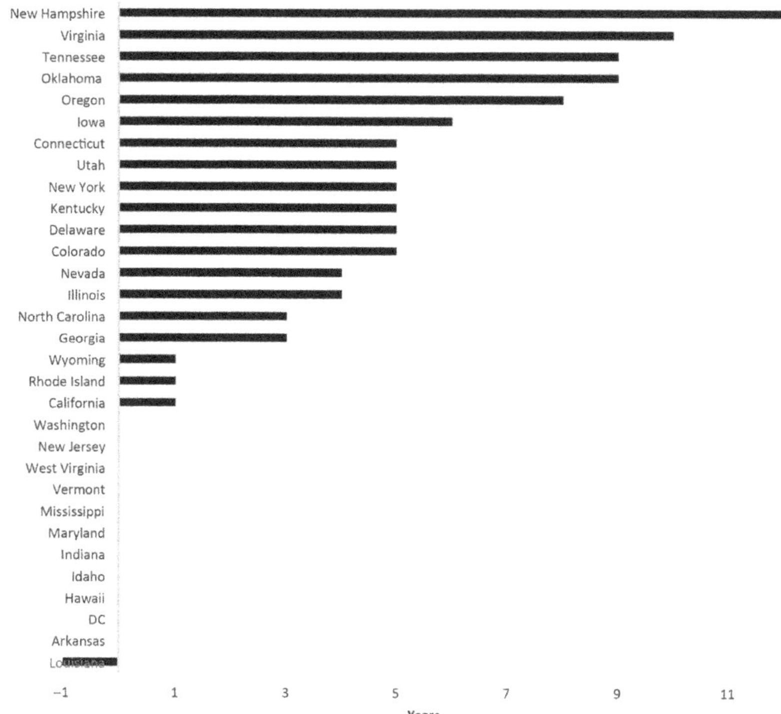

Figure 5.3 Years Before POLST Legislation Adoption.
Source: "National POLST Paradigm Program Designations," National POLST Paradigm, July 6, 2018, http://polst.org/programs-in-your-state/.

POLST has generally remained connected from the right to die debate, but the experiences of advocates in a few states suggest that early legislative involvement can invite political debate or interest group opposition, which can hinder program growth and development. For example, to avoid opposition from the right to life lobby and any connection with the more politically divisive issue of death with dignity, the West Virginia Initiative to Improve End of Life Care had to underscore the fact that POLST use not mandatory.

Programs that existed years before the enactment of legislation reflect an incremental approach to program development. Coalitions in these states established pilot programs and used evidence from these programs to make revisions before expanding the program statewide, government intervention (legislative or regulatory), or clinical acceptance. To develop California's form and process, a statewide coalition piloted programs in seven counties a year before the adoption of state legislation that established POLST use statewide. New York State's MOLST program, which launched in 2001, started using MOLST in hospitals and nursing homes in only the Rochester area, but language in the state's DNR law proved a barrier. Four years later the legislature amended the law, and it could begin piloting the program, which produced the evidence necessary to advocate for legislation that made MOLST permanent and statewide in 2008.

The twenty states that do not appear in figure 5.3 have programs that exist without legislation or administrative regulation.[21] Programs developed and sustained exclusively by clinical consensus afford health care professionals the most autonomy, such as Oregon. However, lack of state involvement generally implies that they have not become statewide but remain concentrated in particular pockets. Programs in these states are educating health care professionals about POLST, conducting research to assess their effectiveness, and providing ongoing training education and quality improvement to increase the likelihood of POLST becoming a standard of care. In states such as Minnesota where significant polarization exists on end life issues, keeping the POLST paradigm out of politics gives health care professionals the opportunity to work collaboratively to design a form based on the best interests of terminally ill patients.

CONCLUSION

In the ongoing quest to recognize and honor patients' health care preferences at the end of life, POLST advances the legal transactional approach by shifting patients' directions to physician orders. While POLST is not a panacea for all the problems that plague advance directives, it represents a distinct improvement upon it. Beyond POLST's purpose, what sets it apart from other end of life policies is the way in which it emerged and how it continues to proliferate. The inclusiveness and cooperative efforts of the Oregon POLST Coalition not only produced a form, it perpetuated a model for policymaking that, for the first time in this policy area, would be led by a coalition of health professionals and would not necessarily require the approval of elected of officials. POLST propagation would require the formulation of a national organization that would guide programs by concentrating on improving education and policy and conducting research to assess the quality and effectiveness.

Over the past twenty-five years, POLST has become a national phenomenon embraced by health professionals in every state and Washington, DC. Still, intrastate dynamics continue to play a significant role in its development and implementation. The variation in program development underscores the complexities involved in instituting a process that is driven by health care professionals and patients. In the end, although states vary widely in their level of adoption and the functionality of their programs, the public's increasing acceptability of POLST compared to death with dignity policies unmasks the many dimension of the concept of patient control and choice.

NOTES

1. Patient Self Determination Act of 1990, 42 U.S.C. § 1395cc.

2. American Hospital Association. 1991. "Directory of Health Care Coalitions in the United States." Chicago: The Hospital.

3. Barbara L. Kass-Bartelmes and Rhonda Hughes, "Advance Care Planning: Preferences for Care at the End of Life," *Journal Pain Palliative Care Pharmacotherapy* 18, no. 1 (August 17, 2009): 87–109.

4. Virginia Code 11-9.1.

5. Peter H. Ditto, William D. Smucker, Joseph H. Danks, Jill A. Jacobson, Renate M. Houts, Angela Fagerilin, Kristen M. Coppola, and Gready, R. Mitchell, "Stability of Older Adults' Preferences for Life-Sustaining Medical Treatment," *Health Psychology* 22, no. 6 (November 2003): 605–15.

6. Since March 2017, the Oregon Task Force has been known as the Oregon POLST Coalition.

7. Oregon POLST Task Force. 1993. "Medical Treatment Coversheet (MTC)." *Center for Ethics in Health Care, Oregon Health Sciences University,* n.d., https://static1.squarespace.com/static/52dc687be4b032209172e33e/t/56da0117746fb9371ddd1cad/1457127713015/Medical+Treatment+Cover+Sheet.pdf.

8. Oregon POLST Task Force."Medical Treatment Coversheet (MTC)." *Center for Ethics in Health Care, Oregon Health Sciences University,* n.d., https://static1.squarespace.com/static/52dc687be4b032209172e33e/t/56da0092b09f956d88f289bb/1457127580888/1995+front+and+back.pdf.

9. Susan W. Tolle, Virginia P. Tilden, Christine A. Nelson, and Patrick M. Dunn, "A Prospective Study of the Efficacy of the Physician Order Form for Life-Sustaining Treatment," *Journal of the American Geriatrics Society* 46, no. 9 (September 1998): 1097–102; Melinda Lee, Kenneth Brummel-Smith, Jan Meyer, Nicholas Drew, and Marla R. London. 2000. "Physician Orders for Life-Sustaining Treatment (POLST): Outcomes in a PACE Program," *Journal of the American Geriatrics Society* 48, no. 10 (October 2000): 1219–25; Terri. A. Schmidt, Susan E. Hickman, Susan W. Tolle, and Health S. Brooks, "The Physician Orders for Life-Sustaining Treatment Program: Oregon Emergency Medical Technicians' Practical Experiences and Attitudes." *Journal of the American Geriatrics Society* 52, no. 9 (September 2004): 1430–34.

10. At the time, state inclusion only required the usage of the POLST Paradigm for a minimal of three years. Because of its affiliation with OHSU, NPPTF founding could only come from private donations or grants. NPPTF's 2015 separation from OHSU made it eligible for health care industry support. In 2017, NPPTF moved to Washington, DC, and is a project of the philanthropic organization, Tides. Tides, "Social Venture: National POLST Paradigm," *Tides*, n.d., https://www.tides.org/project/national-polst-paradigm/.

11. South Dakota may have been later; it is unclear when its program began. Michelle Roy, the Senior Director Community Case Management for Patient Care Services at Rapid City Regional Hospital, told me in an email that a group has been

working on a form for a few years and have recently made progress but has not started using the form (July 7, 2018).

12. National POLST Paradigm, "National POLST Paradigm: POLST Adoption by State," *National POLST Paradigm*, April 24, 2018, http://polst.org/wp-content/uploads/2018/04/2018.04.24-State-POLST-Adoption-Map.pdf.

13. National POLST Paradigm, "National POLST Registry Information," *National POLST Paradigm*, April 10, 2018, http://polst.org/wp-content/uploads/2018/04/2018.04.10-National-POLST-Registry-Information.pdf.

14. National POLST Paradigm, "National POLST Application for Endorsed POLST Paradigm Program Status." *National POLST Paradigm*, July 23, 2015, http://polst.org/wp-content/uploads/2017/10/2015.07.23-Application-for-Endorsed-POLST-Paradigm-Program-Status.pdf.

15. National POLST Paradigm, "Appropriate POLST Paradigm Form Use Policy," *National POLST Paradigm*, April 27, 2018, http://polst.org/wp-content/uploads/2018/04/2018.04.27-Appropriate-Use-of-POLST-Paradigm.pdf.

16. The figure labels Oregon's program as mature; however, in 2017, Oregon POLST Coalition Leaders (formerly known as the Task Force) separated from the National POLST Paradigm organization due to "operational differences."

17. According the National POLST Paradigm website, the Massachusetts MOLST Form does not include the "limited intervention" section and Vermont's form is "cumbersome and unclear." The programs in Nebraska lack form uniformity and consistency, as some of the forms used are not medical orders. Based on legislation passed in 2013 (MD Health Gen. § 5-608.1(c) (2) (i and ii), Maryland requires the completion of the form (with or without the patient's permission) and does not require or even make space available for a patient's signature National POLST Paradigm, "Program Status," April 11, 2018, http://polst.org/wp-content/uploads/2018/04/2018.04.11-POLST-Program-Status.pdf.

18. The National POLST Paradigm Program recently published a more thorough comparison of the legislative differences between POLST Programs at http://polst.org/wp-content/uploads/2018/04/2018.04.29-POLST-Legislative-Comparison-Chart.pdf.

19. LA HB 1485 (2010); AR S.B. 356 (2017); Washington, DC, Act 21-247 (2015); HI HB 1379 (2009); Idaho Code Ann. §§ 39-4512 to -4514 (West 2012) (adopted 2006); IN HB 1182 (2013); MD HB 82 (2011); MS HBZ 1014 (2014); VT Stat. Ann. tit. 18, §§ 9701, 9707, 9709 (West 2012) (adopted 2005, amended 2011); W. Va. Code § 1630-25 (West 2012) (adopted 2002); N.J.S.A. 26:2H-129 through 140 (Approved 2011).

20. See La. Rev. Stat. Ann. § 40:1299.64.2(8); Idaho Code Ann. 39-4512A(4)(c) (2007).

21. The following states have not enacted legislation as of this writing: Alaska, Connecticut, Florida, Kansas, Maine, Massachusetts, Michigan, Minnesota, Missouri, Montana, Nebraska, New Jersey, New Mexico, North Dakota, Pennsylvania, South Carolina, South Dakota, Texas, Washington, and Wisconsin.

Chapter 6

End of Life Polices Today and Tomorrow

During an era in American politics when partisanship, it seems, trumps everything, there appears to be a few exceptions. Medicare reimbursement for end of life consultations, previously proposed as Section 1233 during the ACA health care reform debate, may be one of them. Six years after partisan politics nearly derailed the ACA using false claims of "death panels," in 2015, the Centers for Medicare and Medicaid Services (CMS) introduced a rule virtually identical to the measure Republicans had criticized. It took effect in January 2016.[1] Opposition was muted, Sarah Palin's new Facebook post criticizing the change notwithstanding.[2] Republicans lacked unity on the issue. For example, Jeb Bush expressed some regrets about the bind that Terri Schiavo's case had created for her family. At a campaign event in the course of his presidential nomination bid in April 2015 he suggested that all Medicare recipeints should discuss advance directives with their families to avoid later disagreements.[3] According to Kaiser Health News, during the first year of implementation, nearly 575,000 Medicare beneficiaries participated in end of life conversations with health care providers, nearly twice as many as the American Medical Association had projected.[4] Republican opposition continues; in 2017, US House of Representatives Member Steve King (R-Iowa) introduced the Protecting Life Until Natural Death Act which would prohibit Medicare coverage of advanced planning services, but there has not been any activity on the bill.[5]

At the state level, the role of partisanship varies with respect to POLST programs and to PAD legislation, depending on intrastate political, social, religious, and economic dynamics. Nowhere in the United States has Republican opposition been strong enough to eliminate the POLST Paradigm Program completely. Even so, Catholic organizations and disability rights organizations are the most common opposition to these programs. On the other hand, partisanship plays a huge role in whether PAD legislation exists in US jurisdictions. This chapter discusses about the state of POLST Paradigm Programs and the obstacles they face to full implementation as well as the future of aid in dying adoption and diffusion.

ORGANIZED INTERESTS AGAINST POLST

One in six hospital beds in the United States are in a Catholic hospital system, which gives Catholic organizations enormous influence in the development and sustainability of POLST Paradigm Programs nationwide.[6] Since the 1950s, Catholic doctrine has permitted terminally ill patients to refuse life-sustaining treatment and to request its withdrawal and to refuse extraordinary measures, but not to refuse food or water. The Church deems suicide to avoid a "poor quality of life" a sin against God. The Catholic Medical Association (CMA), the largest association of Catholic physicians, as well as the National Catholic Bioethics Center discourage use of POLST Paradigm. They contend that usage results in premature withdrawal of life-sustaining treatment, which includes any situation when death is not imminent. These groups are influential in the progress and development of POLST programs in Florida, Minnesota, Texas, and Wisconsin. However, in California and Oregon, Catholic health care facilities participate in POLST programs.

The other primary opposition to POLST Paradigm programs, the disability rights community, question whether participation is always voluntary. They have particularly criticized states that do not require patients to sign medical orders. In 2013, the national disability rights group, Not Dead Yet, issued a statement raising concerns about the presentation of the form to disabled patients who may be led to believe they will not be able to live full lives if they choose to receive life-sustaining treatment. That same year, Second Thoughts Connecticut, a disability advocacy group that opposes aid in dying, was successful in blocking HB 6521, An Act Concerning Medical Orders in Life-Sustaining Treatment.[7] In 2014, the organization participated in the drafting of a revised bill that included consumer protections. The Governor signed the measure to establish a pilot program for medical orders for life-sustaining treatment (MOLST) in May 2014.[8]

RECENT DEATH WITH DIGNITY LEGISLATIVE ATTEMPTS

Unlike POLST, death with dignity bills and initiatives have always faced interest group opposition. Only within the last few years, and in a few states, has partisan patterns emerged. Death with dignity bills have generally had Democratic sponsorship, and increasingly, Republican legislators vote against them. Table 6.1 presents death with dignity legislative activity that occurred in 2017 and 2018 legislative sessions. In all, twenty-three states considered Death with Dignity legislation. Democratic legislators introduced nineteen of the bills. Four bills have had bipartisan

Table 6.1 Death with Dignity Legislative Activity 2018/2019 Session as of January 5, 2019.

States with Legal Death with Dignity by Court Decision	*Jurisdictions with a Death with Dignity Statute*	*States Considering Death with Dignity this Year/Session*	*States with No Activity this Year/Session*
Montana	California	Alaska	Alabama
	Colorado	Arizona	Arkansas
	District of Columbia	Connecticut	Florida
	Hawaii	Delaware	Georgia
	Oregon	Indiana	Idaho
	Vermont	Kansas	Illinois
	Washington	Maine	Iowa
		Massachusetts	Kentucky
		Michigan	Louisiana
		Minnesota	Maryland
		Missouri	Mississippi
		Nebraska	Nevada
		New Hampshire	New Mexico
		New Jersey	North Dakota
		New York	South Carolina
		North Carolina	South Dakota
		Ohio	Texas
		Oklahoma	Virginia
		Pennsylvania	West Virginia
		Rhode Island	Wyoming
		Tennessee	
		Utah	
		Wisconsin	

Source: Death with Dignity. 2018. "Take Action in Your State: Death with Dignity Around the US," *Death with Dignity*. https://www.deathwithdignity.org/take-action/ (January 14, 2019).

sponsorship—in Maine, Massachusetts, New Hampshire, and New York.[9] Nebraska State Senator Ernie Chambers (I-North Omaha) is the only independent. While most of the bills have either died or remain in committee for consideration, two of the bipartisan measures, in Maine and Massachusetts, progressed further, perhaps signaling the adoption of the next to death with dignity statutes.

MAINE'S 2017 DEATH WITH DIGNITY BILLS

In February 2017, Maine Republican State Senator Roger Katz (Kennebec/Augusta) along with ten bipartisan co-sponsors from both chambers introduced

SP 113 / LD 347, An Act to Support Death with Dignity.[10] A month later, Jennifer Parker (D–South Berwick) introduced an almost identical, bipartisan bill, HP 749 / LD 1066, An Act to Support Life with Dignity in the Maine House of Representatives.[11] Following a joint hearing of the Health and Human Services (HHS) Committee in April, the committee voted 5 to 8 against the bill with the recommendation "Ought Not to Pass." Six of the eight votes against the bill were Republicans in the House. In May, LD 347 was reported out of the HHS committee with provisions from LD 1066. The combined bill, LD 347, passed the Senate 16 to 15 but the bid ended when the House voted against the bill 61 to 85. However, the It's My Death and Maine Death with Dignity organizations have already planned to put a Death with Dignity initiative on the ballot in November 2019 with the support of the Death with Dignity National Center and the Death with Dignity Political Fund.[12]

MASSACHUSETTS 2017 DEATH WITH DIGNITY BILLS

As in Maine, bipartisan bills entered both chambers in Massachusetts in January 2017. Louis Kafka (D-Stoughton) led a bipartisan effort of 45 representatives in sponsoring H 1194, An Act Relative to End of Life Options while Senator Barbara L'Italien (D-Second Essex and Middlesex) led a bipartisan group of twelve to in sponsoring S 1225, An Act Relative to End of life Option.[13] The Joint Committee on Public Health held a hearing on both bills in September 2017. For the first time, the Massachusetts Medical Society adopted a "neutral engagement on the issue" so that the organization could serve as a medical and scientific resource for the development of the legislation.[14] In spring 2018, the committee sent both bills to study, which ended legislative consideration for the session.[15] Sponsors have expressed commitment to getting the bills on the legislative agenda during the next legislative session.

NEW JERSEY'S 2018–2019 BILLS

Assemblyman John Burzichelli's (D-Gloucester) sponsorship of Aid in Dying for the Terminally Ill Act began in 2012, shortly before the death of his sister, Claudia Burzichelli, from lung cancer in 2013. As support grew over the years among members of his party, the measure faced strong opposition for then Governor Chris Christie, a Republican, who had been vocal about vetoing death with dignity legislation. The election of a democratic governor coupled with increasing approval among voters and state legislators aided in its advancement over the years. January 2018, Senators Nicholas Scutari (D-Union) and Richard Codey (D-27) along with Assemblymembers Joe Danielsen (D-Somerset), and Tim Eustace (D-Bergen) Annette Chaparro (D-33), Jamel Holley (D-20), Mila Jasey (D-27), Angelica Jimenez (D-32), Gordon Johnson (D-37), John McKeon (D-27), and Gabriela Mosquera (D-4) joined Burzichelli in sponsoring the bill.[16] After passing through various committees, both chambers took a floor vote on Mach 25, 2019. The Assembly passed the bill 41 to 33 and the State Senate 21 to 16. Governor Murphy recently issued a statement confirming his intent the sign the bill stating that, “Allowing terminally ill and dying residents thc dignity to make end of life decisions according to their own conscience is the right thing to do.”[17]

CONCLUDING THOUGHTS

Over the last century, the terms, key actors, interest groups, policies, and societal attitudes about aid in dying may have changed for some but the underlying objective of the right to die movement remains centered on choice. As the previous chapters demonstrate, in their ongoing quest to legislate the issue, as a one-sided morality policy, advocates have always faced cultural, religious, and political obstacles, which has resulted in incremental policy diffusion.

A shift in care of the dying in the nineteenth century to physicians that coincided with the rise of anesthetics and narcotics heightened their ethical responsbility. The Hippocratic Oath has ethically obligated physicians to keep patients alive and “do no harm,” but their increased participation in dying expanded the interpretation to include patients deemed incurable. As stories of physicians using pain medication to induce death began to travel outside of medical circles, a national discourse about regulating their authority soon followed. The few who sought reform could not compete with the univerally held belief that doctors were godlike figures so for decades reform efforts ceased.

When it reemerged on a state’s agenda in the 1930s, aid in dying had been usurped by the social Darwinian themes that pervaded the eugenics movement which caused more confusion than policy advocacy or adoption. Even without an active policy agenda or direction, the Roman Catholic Church began to position itself as aid in dying movement’s earliest and most vocal opponent. By 1937, the nation’s flirtation with eugenics resulted in legalized sterilization of the defective (e.g., criminals, prostitutes, imbeciles, feeble-minded people) in thirty-two states. Advocates hoped the formation of Euthanasia Society of America would help to legitimize the cause, but the pervasiveness of eugenics only served to fracture the organization and its reform efforts. The public's growing penchant for eugenics *euthanasia* quickly waned when it became directly responsible for mass murdering by Nazi Germany during World War II which ultimately discredited any use of term *euthanasia* in the United States.

After decades of living in the shadows of eugenics, in the 1960s, the modern right to die movement redefined itself by denouncing all associations with its past while embracing a newfound commitment to promoting policies that enhance patient autonomy at the end of life. Pope Pius XII's permittance of terminally ill patients to refuse life-sustaining treatment and to request its withdrawal opened a new path for the movement that had already began to gain in popularity by advocating for living wills. After several attempts to pass living will legislation during the 1970s, elected officials in California were finally receptive to the laws and thus giving the movement its first legislative victory. Since then, legalistic transactional approaches to end of life planning have diffused without any notable political opposition. As an innovation designed and implemented by clinicians, POLST Paradigm Programs have started in almost every state. Still, the extent to which implementation of the programs occur is often complicated by state regulations and statutes, and political climate that disfavors end of life policymaking outside of legislative reach and oversight. More broadly, advocates continue to rely on the Fourteenth Amendment's due process and equal protection clauses to establish a fundamental right to die as a basic aspect of personal autonomy. In *Cruzan*, the Court clearly found that a competent adults' refusal of medical treatment is a fundamental right.

Decriminalization of aid in dying abroad in the 1970s also breathed new life into the issue at home. It also created an advocacy void that the Hemlock Society would soon fill in the 1980s. By 1992, Hemlock had attracted 57,000 members, established 86 chapters and its newsletter, the *Hemlock Quarterly*, with close to 40,000 subscribers.[18] Its promotion and legal efforts also led to the adoption of the first death with dignity law in Oregon in 1997. Given the groundswell of support and national attention aid in dying had received in the 1990s thanks to Jack Kevorkian, advocates believed other states would quickly follow. Twenty-two years and a mere seven adoptions later, advocates are still waiting. As this book has demonstrated, the one-sidedness of the issue *can* produce opportunities for congruencies between public opinion and legislatively responsiveness, but these events are highly susceptible to timing and elected officials' ideology which essentially makes policy adoption rare occurrences. In each example, adoptions were slow to occur, and to date, have only occurred in states whose statehouses were primarily Democratic and whose voters were mostly white and non-religious. Achieving legislative success outside of this specific demographic requires the movement to permeate the inescapable stronghold of the sanctity of life value system exhibited in the opinions and amicus briefs filed in *Glucksberg*.

The growing participation of political parties has brought about a new dimension to the right to die discourse and policymaking process. In some states this has created deadlock. Only time will tell whether the problem will persist, and party alignment will define end of life policy decision making. Still, because the concept of individual choice has become an indelible feature of death and dying, the question isn't whether to legislate the issue but how.

NOTES

1. Revisions to Payment Policies Under the Physician Fee Schedule and Other Revisions to Part B for CY 2016, CMS-1631-P (2015).
2. Sarah Palin, "Death Panels Still Not Dead." Facebook Post, July 9, 2015, https://www.facebook.com/sarahpalin/posts/10153477582273588.
3. Ed O'Keefe, "Jeb Bush: Maybe Medicare Recipients Should Be Required to Sign Advance Directives." *The Washington Post*, April 17, 2015, https://www.washingtonpost.com/news/post-politics/wp/2015/04/17/jeb-bush-on-terri-schiavo-i-dont-think-i-would-have-changed-anything/?utm_term=.559164566d38.
4. JoNel Aleccia, "End-of-Life Advice: Medicare Covers the Cost of Care-Planning Sessions." *The Seattle Times*, August 14, 2017, https://www.seattletimes.com/nation-world/end-of-life-advice-medicare-covers-the-cost-of-care-planning-sessions/.
5. HR 410, 115 Cong. (January 10, 2017).
6. Somashekhar, Sandhya and Julie Zauzmer, "Report: 1 in 6 Hospital Beds in US is in a Catholic Institution, Restricting Reproductive Rights." *The Washington Post*, May 5, 2016, https://www.washingtonpost.com/news/acts-of-faith/wp/2016/05/05/report-1-in-6-hospital-beds-in-u-s-is-in-a-catholic-hospital-restricting-reproductive-care/?utm_term=.a03b22d496e8.
7. Second Thoughts Connecticut, "Testimony Regarding HB 6521, An Act Concerning Medical Orders for Life-Sustaining Treatment." *Second Thoughts Connecticut*, n.d., https://www.cga.ct.gov/2013/PHdata/Tmy/2013HB-06521-R000315-Mendelsohn,%20Stephen-TMY.PDF.
8. Substitute for Raised SB 413, An Act Concerning the Department of Public Health's Recommendations Regarding Medical Orders for Life-Sustaining Treatment (Connecticut, 2014).
9. SP 113, An Act to Support Death with Dignity (Maine) introduced May 23, 2017; H 1194, An Act Relative to End of Life Options (Massachusetts) introduced January 27, 2017; SB 490, Establishing a Commission to Study End of Life Choices (New Hampshire) introduced January 5, 2018; A02383A, Medical Aid in Dying (New York) introduced January 23, 2018.
10. Senate co-sponsors: Brown Carson (D-Cumberland), Geoff Gratwick (D-Penobscot), Dawn Hill (D-York), Dave Miramant (D-Knox), and Kimberley Rosen (R-Hancock); Representatives co-sponsors: Denise Harlow (D-Portland), Brian Hubbell (D-Bar Harbor), Patricia Hymanson (D-York), Eric Jorgensen (D-Portland), and Stephen Wood (R-Greene).
11. Senate co-sponsors: Ben Chipman (R-Cumberland), Roger Katz (R-Kennebec), and Joyce Maker (R-Washington); Representatives co-sponsors: Jennifer

Parker (D-South Berwick), Mark Bryant (D-Windham), Brian Hubbell (D-Bar Harbor), David McCrea (D-Fort Fairfield), Teresa Pierce (D-Dresden), Maureen Terry (D-Gorham), and Charlotte Warren (D-Hallowell).

12. Death with Dignity National Center, "Maine." *Death with Dignity National Center*, n.d., https://www.deathwithdignity.org/states/maine/.

13. Leonard Mirra (R-Second Essex) is the only Republican to sponsor Senate bill. A complete list of the sponsors is posted at https://malegislature.gov/Bills/190/H1194/Cosponsor. The House bill was sponsored entirely by House Democrats. Co-sponsors of the House bill included William N. Brownsberger (D-Second Suffolk and Middlesex), Patricia D. Jehlen (D-Second Middlesex), Marjorie C. Decker (D-Twenty-Fifth Middlesex) Louis L. Kafka (D-Eighth Norfolk), Cynthia Stone Creem (D-First Middlesex and Norfolk), Jay R. Kaufman (D-Fifteenth Middlesex), Dylan Fernandes (D-Barnstable, Dukes and Nantucket), Ann M. Gobi (D-Worcester, Hampden, Hampshire and Middlesex), Kenneth J. Donnelly (D-Fourth Middlesex), James B. Eldridge (D-Middlesex and Worcester), Julian Cyr (D-Cape and Islands), Peter V. Kocot (D-First Hampshire), Cindy F. Friedman (D-Fourth Middlesex), and Mike Connolly (D-Twenty-Sixth Middlesex).

14. Massachusetts Medical Society, "Massachusetts Medical Society Adopts Several Organizational Policies at Interim Meeting." *Massachusetts Medical Society,* December 2, 2017, http://www.massmed.org/News-and-Publications/MMS-News-Releases/Massachusetts-Medical-Society-adopts-several-organizational-policies-at-Interim-Meeting/#.W3nCuOhKhPY.

15. Colin. A. Young, "Assisted Suicide Bill Dies in Massachusetts Legislature." *Telegram.com,* March 27, 2018, http://www.telegram.com/news/20180327/assisted-suicide-bill-dies-in-massachusetts-legislature.

16. Death with Dignity, "New Jersey." Death with Dignity National Center, n.d., https://www.deathwithdignity.org/states/new-jersey/.

17. Phil Murphy, "Statement from Governor Murphy on Medical Aid in Dying for the Terminally Ill Act." State of New Jersey Governor Phil Murphy, March 25, 2019, https://nj.gov/governor/news/news/562019/approved/20190322d.shtml.

18. Anne Fadiman, "Death News: Requiem for the Hemlock Quarterly." *Harpers* 288, no. 1727 (April 1994): 74–80, 82.

Bibliography

Appel, Jacob M. "A Duty to Kill? A Duty to Die? Rethinking the Euthanasia Controversy of 1906." *Bulletin of the History of Medicine* 78, no. 3 (2004): 610–34.

Ball, Howard. *The Right to Die: A Reference Handbook.* Contemporary World Issues. Santa Barbara, CA: ABC-CLIO, LLC, 2017.

———. *At Liberty to Die: The Battle for Death with Dignity in America.* New York: NYU Press, 2012.

Berry, Frances, and William D. Berry. "State Lottery Adoptions as Policy Innovations: An Event History Analysis." *American Political Science Review* 84, no. 2 (1990): 395–415.

Boushey, Graeme. *Policy Diffusion Dynamics in America.* New York: Cambridge University Press, 2010.

Brown, Barbara A. "The History of Advance Directives. A Literature Review." *Journal of Gerontological Nursing* 29, no. 9 (2003): 4–14.

Burns, J. P., J. Edwards, J. Johnson, N. H. Cassem, and R. D. Truog. "Do-Not-Resuscitate Order after 25 Years." *Critical Care Medicine* 31, no. 5 (2003): 1543–50.

Carson, Rob. "Washington's I-119." *The Hastings Center Report* 22, no. 2 (1992): 7–9.

Catholic Church. *Catechism of the Catholic Church.* Second edition. Vatican: Libreria Editrice, 2000.

Center, Death with Dignity National. "Hawaii." n.d., https://www.deathwithdignity.org/about/history/ (accessed May 8, 2018).

Clark, Nina, and Phoebe S. Liebig. "The Politics of Physician-Assisted Death: California's Proposition 161 and Attitudes of the Elderly." *Politics and the Life Sciences* 15, no. 2 (1996): 273–80.

Bahler, Kristen. "Opinion: Why the Mass. Death with Dignity Act Should Appear on the November Ballot." *TNGG Boston*, January 4, 2012, http://archive.boston.com/lifestyle/blogs/thenextgreatgeneration/2012/01/opinion_why_the_mass_death_wit.html.

Ball, Howard. *The Right to Die: A Reference Handbook.* Contemporary World Issues. Santa Barbara, CA: ABC-CLIO, LLC, 2017.

Baughman, William H., and John C. Bruha. "Euthanasia: Criminal, Tort, Constitutional and Legislative Considerations." *Notre Dame Law Review* 48, no. 5 (1973): 1202–60.

Baxter V. Montana, MT DA 09-0051, 2009 MT 449 (2009).

Browne, William P. "Organized Interests and Their Issue Niches: A Search for Pluralism in a Policy Domain." *Journal of Politics* 52, no. 2 (1990; 1992): 477–509.

Brugger, Christian, Louis C. Breschi, Edith Mary Hart, Mark Kummer, John I. Lane, Peter T. Morrow, Franklin L. Smith, et al. "The POLST Paradigm and Form: Facts and Analysis." *The Linacre Quarterly* 80, no. 2 (2013): 103–38.

Buck V. Bell, 274 U.S. 200 (1927).

Calder, Meta. "Chapter 765 Revisited: Florida's New Advance Directives Law." *Florida State University Law Review* 20 (1992): 291–365.

Childress, Sarah. "The Evolution of America's Right-to-Die Movement." *Frontline*, November 13, 2012, https://www.pbs.org/wgbh/frontline/article/the-evolution-of-americas-right-to-die-movement/.

Cheyfitz, Kirk. "Who Decides? The Connecting Thread of Euthanasia, Eugenics, and Doctor-Assisted Suicide." *OMEGA - Journal of Death and Dying* 40, no. 1 (2000): 5–16.

Connor, Stephen R. "Development of Hospice and Palliative Care in the United States." *OMEGA—Journal of Death and Dying* 56, no. 1 (2008): 89–99.

Crowley, John F. "To Be or Not to Be: Examining the Right to Die; Note." *Journal of Legislation* 18, no. 2 (1992): 347–55.

Dowbiggin, Ian. *A Concise History of Euthanasia: Life, Death, God, and Medicine.* Lanham, MD: Rowman & Littlefield, 2007.

Death with Dignity. "Washington Death with Dignity Act: A History." Death with Dignity, n.d., http://www.deathwithdignity.org/washington-death-with-dignity-act-history/.

Death with Dignity National Center. "Chronology of Assisted Dying." n.d., https://www.deathwithdignity.org/assisted-dying-chronology/ (accessed April 1, 2018).

———. "Death with Dignity in Vermont: History." n.d., www.deathwithdignity.org/death-with-dignity-vermont-history/ (accessed May 16, 2018).

———. "History." n.d., https://www.deathwithdignity.org/about/history/ (accessed May 16, 2018).

DeBonis, Mike. "'Death with Dignity' Bill Likely to Get Slow Walk through DC Council." (2015). https://www.washingtonpost.com/blogs/mike-debonis/wp/2015/02/02/death-with-dignity-bill-likely-to-get-slow-walk-through-d-c-council/?utm_term=.c5090983a101

Dessin, Carolyn L. "Acting as Agent under a Financial Durable Power of Attorney: An Unscripted Role." *University of Akron School of Law* 75, no. 3 (1996): 574–620.

Dowbiggin, Ian. "From Sander to Schiavo: Morality, Partisan Politics, and America's Culture War over Euthanasia, 1950–2010." *Journal of Policy History* 25, no. 1 (2013): 12–41.

———. *A Concise History of Euthanasia: Life, Death, God, and Medicine*. Lanham, MD: Rowman & Littlefield, 2007.

———. *A Merciful End: The Euthanasia Movement in Modern America.* Oxford: Oxford University Press, 2003.

Emanuel, E. J., B. D. Onwuteaka-Philipsen, J. W. Urwin, and J. Cohen. "Attitudes and Practices of Euthanasia and Physician-Assisted Suicide in the United States, Canada, and Europe." *Jama* 316, no. 1 (2016): 79–90.

Emanuel, Ezekiel J. "The History of Euthanasia Debates in the United States and Britain." *Annals of Internal Medicine* 121 (1994): 793–802.

Euthanasia Research & Guidance Organization (ERGO). "About Derek Humphry." 2018(2010). www.finalexit.org/about_derek_humphry.html#career.

Fagerlin, Angela, and Carl E. Schneider. "Enough: The Failure of the Living Will." *The Hastings Center Report* 34, no. 2 (2004): 30–42.

Fine, Robert L. "From Quinlan to Schiavo: Medical, Ethical, and Legal Issues in Severe Brain Injury." *Proceedings (Baylor University. Medical Center)* 18, no. 4 (2005): 303–10.

Friedman, Lawrence M. *Crime without Punishment: Aspects of the History of Homicide*. Cambridge, UK and New York: Cambridge University Press, 2018.

Gabriel, Trip. "A Fight to the Death." *The New York Times*, December 8, 1991, https://www.nytimes.com/1991/12/08/magazine/a-fight-to-the-death.html.

Garrow, David J. "The Right to Die: Death with Dignity in America." *Mississippi Law Journal* 68 (1998): 407–30.

Giovanni, Lisa A. "End-of-Life Care in the United States: Current Reality and Future Promise - a Policy Review." *Nursing Economics* 30, no. 3 (2012): 127–34.

Glick, Henry R. *The Right to Die: Policy Innovation and Its Consequences*. New York: Columbia University Press, 1992.

———. "The Right-to-Die: State Policymaking and the Elderly." *Journal of Aging Studies* 5, no. 3 (1991): 283–307.

Glick, Henry R. and Amy Hutchinson. "Physician-Assisted Suicide: Agenda Setting and the Elements of Morality Policy." In *The Public Clash of Private Values : The Politics of Morality Policy*, edited by Christopher Z. Mooney. New York: Chatham House, 2001.

Gorsuch, Neil M. *The Future of Assisted Suicide and Euthanasia*. Princeton, NJ: Princeton University Press, 2006.

Gostin, Lawrence O. "Drawing a Line between Killing and Letting Die: The Law, and Law Reform, or Medically Assisted Dying." *The Journal of Law, Medicine, and Ethics* 21 (1993): 94–101.

Gray, Virginia. "Innovation in the States: A Diffusion Study." *The American Political Science Review* 67, no. 4 (1973): 1174–85.

Gray, Virginia, and David Lowery. "State Interest Group Research and the Mixed Legacy of Belle Zeller." *State Politics and Policy Quarterly* 2, no. 4 (2002): 388–410.

Griswold V. Connecticut, 381 479 (1965).

Haider-Markel, Donald P., and Kenneth J. Meier. "The Politics of Gay and Lesbian Rights: Expanding the Scope of Salience." *The Journal of Politics* 58, no. 2 (1996): 332–49.

Hamedy, Saba. "New Mexico Judge Affirms Right to 'Aid in Dying.'" *Los Angeles Times*, January 19, 2014, www.articles.latimes.com/2014/jan/19/nation/la-na-new-mexico-aid-dying-20140120.

Hamel, Liz, Bryan Wu, and Mollyann Brodie. "Views and Experiences with End-of-Life Medical Care in the US" (2017). http://files.kff.org/attachment/Report-Views-and-Experiences-with-End-of-Life-Medical-Care-in-the-US.

Heinz, John P., Edward O. Laumann, Robert H. Salisbury, and Robert L. Nelson. "Inner Circles or Hollow Cores: Elite Networks in National Policy Systems." *Journal of Politics* 52, no. 2 (1990): 356–90.

Hickman, Susan E., Charles P. Sabatino, Alvin H. Moss, and Jessica Wehrle Nester. "The POLST (Physician Orders for Life-Sustaining Treatment) Paradigm to Improve End-of-Life Care: Potentional State Legal Barriers to Implementation." *Journal of Law, Medicine and Ethics* (2008): 119–40.

Hillyard, Daniel, and John Dombrink. *Dying Right: The Death with Dignity Movement.* New York: Routledge, 2001.

Hirsch, Dana Elizabeth. "Euthanasia: Is It Murder or Mercy Killing? A Comparison of the Criminal Laws in the United States, the Netherlands and Switzerland." *Loyola of Los Angeles International and Comparative Law Review* 12, no. 3 (1990): 821–43.

Humphry, Derek. *Final Exit: The Practicalities of Self-Deliverance and Assisted Suicide for the Dying.* Third edition. New York: Dell Publishing, 2002.

Humphry, Derek, and Ann Wickett. *The Right to Die: Understanding Euthanasia.* First Perennial Library edition. New York: Harper & Row, 1986.

Humphry, Derek, and Mary Clement. *Freedom to Die: People, Politics, and the Right-to-Die Movement.* First edition. New York: St. Martin's Press, 2000.

Humphry, Derek, and Stephen Jamison. *Good Life, Good Death: The Memoir of a Right to Die Pioneer.* New York: Carrel Books, 2017.

In Re Quinlan, 70 N.J. 10; 355 A.2d 647 (1976).

Johnson, Charles S. "Column: Alberton Woman Testified Passionately for Right to Die." *Missoulian* (2009). http://missoulian.com/news/state-and-regional/column-alberton-woman-testified-passionately-for-right-to-die/article_08923b30-8f9e-11de-882b-001cc4c002e0.html.

Johnson, Karen Lowe. "Health Care Coalitions: An Emerging Force for Change." *Hospital & Health Services Administration* 38, no. 4 (1993): 557–69.

Johnson, Tanya F. *Handbook on Ethical Issues in Aging.* Edited by Keith Rollin Eakins. Westport, CT: Greenwood Press, 1999.

John-Stevens, Norman St. "Life, Death and the Law: Law and Christian Morals in England and the United States." Washington, DC: Beard Books, 1961.

Jonsen, Albert R. "Dying Right in California—the Natural Act." *Clinical Toxicology* 13, no. 4 (1978): 513–22.

Kamisar, Yale. "Some Non-Religious Views against Proposed 'Mercy-Killing' Legislation Part I." *Human Life Review* 2, no. 2 (1976): 71–114.

———. "Why Did Voters Reject Michigan's Physician-Assisted Suicide Initiative?" *Law Quad. Notes* 42 (1999): 43.

Kingdon, John W. "Agendas, Alternatives, and Public Policies." In *Classics of Public Policy*, edited by Jay M. Shafritz, Karen S. Layne, and Christopher P. Borick, 148–58. London: Pearson Longman International, 1995.

Lambert, Lane. "Question 2 Sponsors Say Measure Isn't 'Assisted Suicide.'" *The Patriot Ledger* (2012). http://www.patriotledger.com/article/20121016/NEWS/310169744.

Larson, Edward J., and Thomas A. Eaton. "The Limits of Advance Directives: A History and Assessment of the Patient Self-Determination Act." *Wake Forest Law Review* 32 (1997): 249–93.

Lavi, Shai J. *The Modern Art of Dying*. Princeton, NJ: Princeton University Press, 2005.

Lewis, Milton James. *Medicine and Care of the Dying: A Modern History*. New York: Oxford University Press, 2007.

Lopes, Giza. *Dying with Dignity*. Global Crime and Justice. Edited by Graeme R. Newman. Santa Barbara, CA: Praeger, 2015.

McGreevy, Patrick. "After Struggling, Jerry Brown Makes Assisted Suicide Legal in California." *Los Angeles Times*, October 5, 2015, http://www.latimes.com/local/political/la-me-pc-gov-brown-end-of-life-bill-20151005-story.html.

McLaughlin, Catherine G., Wendy K. Zellers, and Lawrence D. Brown. "Health Care Coalitions: Characteristics, Activities, and Prospects." *Inquiry* 26, no. 1 (1989): 72–83.

Meier, Kenneth J. "Drugs, Sex, Rock, and Roll: A Theory of Morality Politics." *Policy Studies Journal* 27, no. 4 (1999): 681–95.

Messinger, Thane Josef. "A Gentle and Easy Death: From Ancient Greece to Beyond Cruzan toward a Reasoned Legal Response to the Societal Dilemma of Euthanasia." *Denver University Law Review* 71 (1993): 175–251.

Mooney, Christopher Z., and Mei-Hsien Lee. "The Influence of Values on Consensus and Contentious Morality Policy: US Death Penalty Reform, 1956–1982." *The Journal of Politics* 62, no. 1 (2000): 223–39.

Morehouse, Sarah M. "Interest Groups, Parties and Politics in the American States." In *the annual meeting of the American Political Science Association*. Washington, DC, 1997.

Morris V. Brendanburg, 376 P.3d 842 (2016).

Norton, Michael J., and Natalie L. Decker. "Suicide by Doctor: What Colorado Would Risk on the Slippery Slope of Physician-Assisted Suicide." no. 2016–1 (2016): 22. http://www.ccu.edu/centennial/wp-content/uploads/2015/01/Suicide-By-Doctor-Policy-Brief-2016-Update.pdf.

Ollove, Michael. "New End-of-Life Measure Quietly Sweeps the Nation." *Stateline*, June 20, 2013, http://www.pewtrusts.org/nb/research-and-analysis/blogs/stateline/2013/06/20/new-endoflife-measure-quietly-sweeps-the-nation.

Olson, Mancur. *The Logic of Collective Action: Public Goods and the Theory of Groups*. Harvard Economic Studies. Cambridge, MA: Harvard University Press, 1965.

Oregon POLST. "POLST History Timeline." http://oregonpolst.org/history-timeline/.

Otlowski, Margaret. *Voluntary Euthanasia and the Common Law*. New York: Oxford University Press, 2000.

Pappas, Demetra M. *The Euthanasia/Assisted-Suicide Debate*. Santa Barbara, CA: Greenwood, 2012.

Partnership for Caring (PFC). "Partnership for Caring (PFC): America's Voices for the Dying." http://www.partnershipforcaring.org/HomePage/.

Patient Choices Vermont. "About PCV - History." *Patient Choices Vermont* (n.d.). www.patientchoices.org/history.html.

Patients Rights Council. "Assisted Suicide and Death with Dignity: Past, Present and Future, Part I." 2017 (2005). http://www.patientsrightscouncil.org/site/rpt2005-part1/.

———. "Assisted Suicide and Death with Dignity: Past, Present and Future, Part I." 2017 (2005). http://www.patientsrightscouncil.org/site/rpt2005-part1/.

PBS. "Chronology of Dr. Jack Kevorkian's Life and Assisted Suicide Campaign." *PBS* (n.d.), www.pbs.org/wgbh/pages/frontline/kevorkian/chronology.html.

Perkins, Henry S. "Controlling Death: The False Promise of Advance Directives." *Annals of Internal Medicine* 147 (2007): 51–57.

Physician Orders for Life-Sustaining Treatment (POLST) Paradigm. "Programs in Your State." *POLST* (n.d.), http://www.polst.org/programs-in-your-state/.

Pew Research Center. "Views on End-of-Life Medical Treatments." Pew, November 21, 2013, http://www.pewforum.org/2013/11/21/views-on-end-of-life-medical-treatments/.

Pope, Thaddeus Mason. "Dangerous Catholic Attack on POLST." In *End of Life*: Bioethics.net, 2013.

Pope, Thaddeus Mason, and Melinda Hexum. "Legal Briefing: POLST: Physician Orders for Life-Sustaining Treatment." *The Journal of Clinical Ethics* 23, no. 4 (2012): 353–57.

Right to LIfe of Michigan. "Proposal B: Ballot Proposal on Assisted Suicide." Right to LIfe of Michigan, https://www.rtl.org/prolife_issues/propb_1998.html.

Robinson, Daniel H., and Alexander H. Toledo. "Historical Development of Modern Anesthesia." *Journal of Investigative Surgery* 25, no. 3 (2012): 141–49.

Russell, O. Ruth. *Freedom to Die: Moral and Legal Aspects of Euthanasia.* Revised edition. New York: Human Sciences Press, 1975.

Quill, Timothy E. "Death and Dignity." *New England Journal of Medicine* 324, no. 10 (1991): 691–94.

———. *Death and Dignity: Making Choices and Taking Charge.* New York: W.W. Norton & Company, 1993.

Right to Life of Michigan. "Chronology of Events Relating to Assisted Suicice and Euthanasia in Michigan." 2018. https://www.rtl.org/legislation/ProlifeLaws/assistedsuicide_chronology.html.

Sabatino, Charles P. "The Evolution of Health Care Advance Planning Law and Policy." *The Milbank Quarterly* 88, no. 2 (2010): 211–39.

———. "Survey of State Ems-Dnr Laws and Protocols." News release, 1999.

Sabatino, Charles P., and Naomi Karp. "Improving Advanced Illness Care: The Evolution of State POLST Programs." Report for POLST, April 2011. https://assets.aarp.org/rgcenter/ppi/cons-prot/POLST-Report-04-11.pdf.

Sackett, Walter F. "Death with Dignity." *Southern Medical Journal* 64 (1971): 330–32.

Schattschneider, E. E. *The Semisovereign People: A Realist's View of Democracy in America.* Hinsdale, IL: The Dryden Press, 1975.

———. *Party Government.* American Government in Action Series. New York, New York: Farrar and Rinehart, 1942.

Schanker, David R. "Of Suicide Machines, Euthanasia Legislation, and the Health Care Crisis." *Indiana Law Journal* 68, no. 3 (1993): 977–1010.

Schiefelbein, Joshua, Zach Markovich, and Avery Feingold. "POLST Registries: Supporting End of Life Decision Making Presented to the New Hampshire House of Representatives, Committee on Heath, Human Services and Elderly Affairs." *Policy Research Shop* (2014): 1–25. https://rockefeller.dartmouth.edu/sites/rockefeller.drupalmulti-prod.dartmouth.edu/files/prs_brief_1314-03.pdf.

Schlozman, Kay Lehman, and John T. Tierney. *Organized Interests and American Democracy.* New York: Harper & Row, 1986.

Sonderling, Keith E. "POLST: A Cure for the Common Advance Directive—It's Just What the Doctor Ordered." *Nova Law Review* 33, no. 2 (2009): 451–80.

Span, Paula. "How the 'Death with Dignity' Initiative Failed in Massachusetts." *New York Times*, December 6, 2012, https://newoldage.blogs.nytimes.com/2012/12/06/how-the-death-with-dignity-law-died-in-massachusetts/.

Spann, Jeri. "Implementing End-of-Life Treatment Preferences across Clinical Settings." *State Initiatives in End-of-Life Care* (1999). https://static1.squarespace.com/static/52dc687be4b032209172e33e/t/570c20669f72664c492701a0/1460412527409/State+Initiatives+in+End+of+Life+Care+April+1999.pdf.

The Washington Post. *Landmark: The inside Story of America's New Health Care Law and What It Means for Us All.* New York: Public Affairs, 2010.

Sunstein, Cass R. "Right to Die, The." *University of Chicago Law School* 106 (1996): 1123.

Thurman, Virgil. "Euthanasia: The Physician's Liability." *The John Marshall Law Review* 10, no. 1 (1976): 148–72.

Tobler, Laura. "Planning for End-of-Life Care." *Legisbrief* 18, no. 34 (2010).

Truman, David B. *The Governmental Process: Political Interests and Public Opinion.* First edition. New York: Knopf, 1951.

Urofsky, Melvin I. "Leaving the Door Ajar: The Supreme Court and Assisted Suicide." *University of Richmond Law Review* 32, no. 2 (1998): 313–405.

Walker, Jack L. *Mobilizing Interest Groups in America: Patrons, Professional, and Social Movements.* Ann Arbor: University of Michigan Press, 1991.

———. "The Origins and Maintenance of Interest Groups in America." *American Political Science Review* 77, no. 2 (1983): 390–406.

———."The Diffusion of Innovations among the American States." *American Political Science Review* 68, no. 3 (1969): 880–99.

Walters, Jonathan. "Boomers Want Control of Their End-of-Life Care." *Governing* (October 2012). Published electronically March 9, 2015, http://www.governing.com/topics/health-human-services/gov-end-of-life-care-control.html.

The Washington Post Editorial Board. "Make the District a Place to Die with Dignity." *The Washington Post*, October 1, 2016, https://www.washingtonpost.com/opinions/make-the-district-a-place-to-die-with-dignity/2016/10/01/e7cca922-84e5-11e6-92c2-14b64f3d453f_story.html?utm_term=.3fadde0ec380.

Washington v. Glucksberg, 521 702 (1997).

Whitney, Leon Fradley. *The Case for Sterilization.* New York: Frederick A. Stokes Company, 1934.

Wiggam, Albert Edward. *The New Decalogue of Science.* Indianapolis, IN: Bobbs-Merrill, 1923.

Wilson, James Q. *Political Organizations.* New York: Basic Books, 1974.

Winslade, William J. "Thoughts on Technology and Death: An Appraisal of California's Natural Death Act." *DePaul Law Review* 26, no. 4 (1977): 717–42.

Yadav, Kuldeep N., Nicole B. Gabler, Elizabeth Cooney, Saida Kent, Jennifer Kim, Nicole Herbst, Adjoa Mante, Scott D. Halpern, and Katherine R. Courtright. "Approximately One in Three Us Adults Completes Any Type of Advance Directive for End-of-Life Care." *Health Affairs* 36, no. 7 (2017): 1244–51.

Yardley, William. "Booth Gardner Dies at 76: Ex-Washington Governor." *New York Times*, March 19, 2013, https://www.nytimes.com/2013/03/19/us/booth-gardner-dies-at-76-ex-washington-governor.html.

Yuen, Jacqueline K., M. Carrington Reid, and Michael D. Fetters. "Hospital Do-Not-Resuscitate Orders: Why They Have Failed and How to Fix Them." *Journal of General Internal Medicine* 26, no. 7 (2011): 791–97.

Ziegler, Mary. *Beyond Abortion: Roe V. Wade and the Battle for Privacy.* Cambridge, MA: Harvard University Press, 2018.

Index

AAHS. *See* Americans Against Human Suffering
abortion, xxi, 9
ACA. *See* Patient Protection and Affordable Care Act
accidents, 7
ACLU. *See* American Civil Liberties Union
Adler, Felix, 1
adoption: end of life policy and, 11–26; legislation and, *87*; of PAD, 32; by states, 18–22
advance directives, 82; discussion of, 91; POLST and, *83*
advocacy, 2, 3, 5; experiences and, 86; policy and, 12; VELS and, 33
aging, xiii
aid in dying, xviii; California and, 15; data on, 18–26; discourse on, 4, 32; patient's rights and, 54; policy and, 1–9. *See also* physician aid in dying
AIDS, 68
AMA. *See* American Medical Association
amendments, 7
American Civil Liberties Union (ACLU), 69
American culture, xiii
American Medical Association (AMA), 36
Americans Against Human Suffering (AAHS), 41
Angell, Lester W., 44
Arkansas, 84
Armstrong, Deborah, 72
Ashcroft, John, 42
Atkins, Janet, 77
autonomy, 88

ballot initiative campaigns, 41–42
bans, 70–72
Barber, Neil L., *57*
Baxter v. Montana, 70
beliefs, 2; shared interests and, 34–35
bills, 2–3, 15, 17, 27n12, 45, 71; death with dignity and, 92–94
Blazer, Harold, *57*
Blewett, Anders, 71
Bower, Muriel, 17
Braunsdorf, Eugene, 55
Breyer, Stephen, 68–69
Brown, Jerry, 13, 15
Buckingham, F. N., 4
Bush, George W., 67

California: aid in dying bills, 15; Gallup polls and, 11
California Medical Association (CMA), 13, 15

capital punishment, xxi, 9
Caraccio, Donald, 58
cardiopulmonary resuscitation (CPR), xv, 81
care, 55; policy and planning, 79–81; standards for, 83, 84
Carrizales, *58*
Catholic Church, 6, 14, 15, 17, 38, 64, 67, 96
Catholic Medical Association (CMA), 92
causation, 56
CFD. *See* Concern for Dying
chloroform, 3, 4, *57*
CID. *See* Compassion in Dying
CMA. *See* California Medical Association; Catholic Medical Association
coalitions, xv, xxiii, 2, 7, 14, 26; health care and, 73, 77–89
Colorado, 13, 14, 15; Proposition 106 in, *16*, *21*, *93*
communication, xv; about DNR, 81; treatment and, 78
Compassion in Dying (CID), 43, 45, 50n27, 67
Comstock, John H., 5–6
Concern for Dying (CFD), 39
conflict, xx–xxi
Connecticut, 48nn5–6
consensus, xii; morality and, 21; programs and, 88
context, xv–xix
countries, *xvii*, xviii
court cases, xxi, 64; interests groups and, 75n31; Kevorkian and, 74nn13–14. *See also specific court cases*
the courts, 52–73; lobbies and, 45
CPR. *See* cardiopulmonary resuscitation
criminalization, 53
Cruzan v. Director, Missouri Department of Health, 64, 65, 66; privacy and, 72; states and, 73
culture, xiii, 83
Dargis, Marilyn, *58*
data, 43; on aid in dying, 18–26
DC. *See* District of Columbia
death, 66–67; care after, 55; defectiveness and, 2; discourse on, 38; experiences and, 9; policy and, 13–18; politics and, xi–xxii; terminology and, xxiii
death with dignity, 27n10; bills and, 92, *93*, 94; legislation about, xiii–xiv; legislation and, 92, *93*, 94; United States and, *xvi–xvii*
decriminalization, 95; of PAD, 11, 13
Democrats, 95
demographics, 95, xxvin32; utilization and, *23–25*
diagnosis, 71
dialogue, 82, 85
discourse, 56, 67, 94; aid in dying as, 4, 32; death in, 38; eugenics in, 6
District of Columbia (DC), 16–17
DNR. *See* do not resuscitate order
doctors. *See* physicians
documentation, 81; physicians and, 82
do not resuscitate order (DNR), 66; communication about, 81
DPAHC. *See* durable power of attorney for health care
Dunn, Patrick, 77, 84
durable power of attorney for health care (DPAHC), 80
dying: expenses and, xiii; organizations aid in, xviii

education, 83
EEC. *See* Euthanasia Education Council
EEF. *See* Euthanasia Educational Fund
Egbert, Lawrence, *60–61*
end of life policy, 91–97; adoption of, 11–26; public opinion and, xix–xx
Engler, John, 63
ESA. *See* Euthanasia Society of America
eugenics, 94; discourse in, 6; women and, 34
eugenics euthanasia, 2

euthanasia, xiii, xiv
Euthanasia Educational Fund (EEF), 38
Euthanasia Education Council (EEC), 31–32, 38
Euthanasia Society of America (ESA), 6, 31; formation of, 32–34; legacy of, 39; Mitchell and, 35; World War II and, 36–37
expenses, xiii
experiences, 1, 3; advocacy and, 86; death and, 9

FCC. *See* Florida Catholic Conference
feedback, 84
Fletcher, Joseph, 38–39, 48n11, 48n13
Florida Catholic Conference (FCC), 8

Gallup polls, xx; California and, 11
Gandhi, Mohandas, 1, 9n1
Gardner, Booth, 14, 22, 27n7
Garrett, Valery, 47n2
Gingrich, Newt, xi
Ginsburg, Ruth Bader, 68–69
Goldstein, Sidney, 35
Gonzales v. Oregon, 42
Greer, George, 66
Gregory, Ross H., 4
Griesa, Thomas P., 68
Griswold v. Connecticut, 65
Grossman, Howard, 68

Haiselden, Harry J., 31
Hall, Anna, 3, 4, *19*
Harris, Andy, 17
Hassman, Joseph, 58
Hawaii, 29n31; PAD in, 17–18
Health and Human Services Committee (HHS), 93
health care, 77–89
Hemlock Society, 15, 39, 50n29; founders of, 32; origins of, 40–41
HHS. *See* Health and Human Services Committee
The Hippocratic Oath, xi–xii, 17, *20*
history, 14; CPR, 81; eugenics and, 34; legislation and, xxiii; opinion and, 69
hospice care, 14, 38, xxvn22
Humphry, Derek, 32, 40, 49n16, 49n19
Humphry, Jean, 40
Hunt, Henry T., 3

illness, 78
implications, 43; World War II and, 36
indictments, 55, 63; physicians and, *57–62*
infanticide, 56
influence, 79
innovation, 95; policy and, 78
In Re Quinlan (1976), xxi
insurance, 16
interest groups, 31–47; briefs filed by, 75n36; court cases and, 75n31; patient's rights and, 54
Iowa, 4
issues, 88; distortion of, xii; ownership of, xxi; unity and, 91

Johnson, Harry C., 55

Kalili, Ali, 63
Kaufman, Richard, 63
Keene, Barry, 12, 27n3
Kerns, Krayton, 71
Kevorkian, Jack, 42, 49n22; court cases and, 74nn13–14; defense and, 63; machines by, 74n8; mercy killing and, 56; Merian's Friends and, 43, 49n23; sentence for, 64
Kraai, John, *57*
Kutner, Luis, 79

lawsuits, 67; states and, 70. *See also* court cases
legislation, 28n15, 79; adoption and, *87*; bills and, 3, 15, 27n12, 71; death with dignity, xiii–xiv; death with dignity and, 92, *93*, 94; enactment of, 87; history and, xxiii; living

wills and, 12–13; Montana and, 8–9; Oregon and, 26; reforms and, 11; regulations, 86; right to die and, 2–6; states and, 53, 54, 74n12
Lepore, Jill, xxii
letters, 3
living wills, 79–80; legislation and, 12–13
Lou Gehrig's disease, 63

Maine, 43–44; death with dignity bills in, 93
Massachusetts, 44–45; death with dignity bills in, 93–94
Maynard, Brittany, 14
McCall, Tom, 8
McCamley, Bill, 72
McCarter, Dorothy, 70
McCaughey, Betsy, xii
media, 56
Medicaid, 44
Medical Orders for Life-Sustaining Treatment (MOLST), 85, 88, 92
Medical Treatment Coversheet (MTC), 82
Medicare Prescription Drug, Improvement, and Modernization Act (2003), xii
memoir, 40
mercy killing, 37, 53; Kevorkian and, 42, 56
Merian's Friends, 43, 49n23
Merrifield, Michael, 16
Michigan, 63
Millard, Charles Killick, 33
Miner, Roger, 68
Mitchell, Ann, 31; ESA and, 35
models, 33
MOLST. *See* Medical Orders for Life-Sustaining Treatment
Montana, 8–9, 70
Montemarano, Vincent, *57*
Moore, Hugh, 39, 48n12
morality, xix; consensus and, 21; policy and, xx–xxii
movements, 38, 47. *See also specific movements*
MTC. *See* Medical Treatment Coversheet

Nagle, Herman, 55
Naramore, Stan, *59*
Nash, Nan, 71
National Council for Death and Dying (NCDD), 39
The National Death Act, 13
National Society for the Legalization of Euthanasia (NSLE), 33
NCDD. *See* National Council for Death and Dying
Nejdl, Robert J., *57*
Neo-pluralism, 36–37
New York, 68
NSLE. *See* National Society for the Legalization of Euthanasia

ObamaCare. *See* Patient Protection and Affordable Care Act
OHSU. *See* Oregon Health and Science University
Oregon, 8, 13; Ballot Measure 16 in, 42–43; legislation in, 26; PAD in, 41
Oregon Health and Science University (OHSU), 77
organizations, 46; aid in dying, xviii; development of, 82–85; merger of, 39; policy and, 47; against POLST, 92

PAD. *See* physician aid in dying
Paight, Carol, 37, 48n5
Palin, Sarah, xi, 91, 96n2; Facebook posts by, xii
palliative care, 14, 38, *60*
Parkinson's disease, 27n7
partisanship, 91
Patient Choices Vermont, 46
Patient Protection and Affordable Care Act (ACA), xi, xii

patients: aid in dying and, 2, 4; doctor and, 53; POLST for, 78; preferences for, 81; Vermont and, 45–46
Patient Self-Determination Act (PSDA), xi, 77
patient's rights, 54; treatment and, 64–65
Pennsylvania, 80
perspective, 34; interest groups and, 46; neo-pluralism as, 36; transactional/economic, 40
Philbrick, Inez Celia, 5
physician aid in dying (PAD), xiv; adoption of, 32; decriminalization of, 13; Hawaii and, 17–18; Kevorkian and, 56; in Oregon, 41; in Switzerland, xviii; terminal illness and, 43–44; United States and, *xvi–xvii*; waiting periods and, xix
Physician Orders for Life-Sustaining Treatment (POLST), 26; advance directives and, *83*; designations for, *86*; form for, xv, 78; national landscape and, 85–88; organizations against, 92; paradigm for, xiv–xv, *84*, 89n10, 90n17; states and, 84, 96–97
physicians, 4, 67; documentation and, 82; indictments for, *57–62*
Pinzon-Reyes, Ernesto, *59*
Pius XII (Pope), 38, 47, 48n8, 95
planning, 79–81
policy: advocacy and, 12; care planning and, 79–81; death and, 13–18; distortion of, xii; entrepreneurs in, 1–9; innovation in, 78; morality and, xx–xxii; organizations and, 47. *See also specific policy*
politics, xi–xxii
POLST. *See* Physician Orders for Life-Sustaining Treatment
Potter, Charles Francis, 31
Pou, Anna, 60
prescription drugs: dying and, xviii; lethal medications and, 26, 27n11
privacy, 65, 72
process, 84
programs, 85–88; coalitions and, 87; consensus and, 88; POLST designations for, *86*
protocol design, 82–85
PSDA. *See* Patient Self-Determination Act
public opinion, 12; end of life policy and, xix–xx

Quill, Timothy, 68
Quinlan, Karen, xxi, 9, 27n1; case of, 11, 74n16

reforms, 11; euthanasia and, xiv
regulations, 86
Republicans, xi–xii, 21, 71, 91
research, 80; CPR and, 81; on POLST, 83
Riggs, Aja, 71
right to die movement, xxiii; fight for, 66–70; legislation and, 2–6
Risley, Robert, 41
Roberts, Frank, 54–55
Robert Wood Johnson Foundation (RWJR), 39, 48n14
Roe v. Wade, 65
Rosier, Peter, *58*
Rothstein, Barbara, 45
RWJR. *See* Robert Wood Johnson Foundation

Sackett, Walter W., 7, 8
Sander, Hermann, 37, *57*
Schaeffer, Richard, *58*
Schiavo, Michael, 66, 73
Schiavo, Terri, 66, 73
Schindler, Mary, 66, 73
Schindler, Robert, 66, 73
Shumlin, Peter, 46, 51n42
society, 35
Society for the Right to Die (SRD), 6
South Dakota, 90n11
SRD. *See* Society for the Right to Die

states, 73, 90n11, 90n21; adoption by, 18–22; bans and, 70–72; DPAHC and, 80; legislation and, 53, 54, 74n12; POLST and, 84, 96–97; programs in, 85, 86
statutes, 86
Stefanics, Elizabeth, 72
sterilization, 5
suicide, xx; Wickett, 47
Switzerland, xviii

Taylor, Pauline, 38
terminal illness, 16; PAD and, 43–44
terminology, xx; death and, xxiii
theories, 1, 5
Three Streams Theory, 1, 6
treatment: communication about, 78; patient's rights and, 64–65
Tschida, Brad, 71

United States: context and, xv–xix; death with dignity in, *xvi–xvii*; hospice care in, xxvn22. *See also specific states*

Vacco v. Quill, 51n37, 69, 75n27
VELS. *See* Voluntary Euthanasia Legalization Society
verdicts, 55
Vermont, 51n41; patient choice in, 45–46
VESC. *See* Voluntary Euthanasia Society of Connecticut
Virginia, 80
Voluntary Euthanasia Legalization Society (VELS), 33
Voluntary Euthanasia Society of Connecticut (VESC), 37
voters, 14

Walters, Ginny, 46
Walters, Richard "Dick," 46
wards of state, 7
Washington, 14, 27n9
Washington v. Glucksberg (1997), xxii, 45, 69
Weitzel, Robert, A., *60*
Wenstrup, Brad, 17
Wickett, Ann, 32, 40; suicide of, 47
women, 5; eugenics and, 34
Wood, Douglas, *59*
World War II, 35; ESA and, 36–37

About the Author

Bianca Easterly is currently assistant professor in the Department of Political Science at Lamar University in Beaumont, Texas. She received a PhD in political science from the University of Houston, and BA and Master of Public Administration (MPA) degrees from the University of Illinois at Chicago. Before her doctoral studies, Easterly spent several years working in both the private and public sectors including the Department of Veterans Affairs Health Services Research and Development (HSR&D) Service. Easterly's interests include American and state institutions and politics, public policy, federalism and intergovernmental relations, and judicial process and behavior. Her research broadly explores morality policies and the political institutions that enhance elite responsiveness to public opinion. Her work appears in *Policy Studies Journal, Law & Policy*, and *Social Science Quarterly*. As an invited columnist for *PA Times Online*, she has written about a variety of topics related to the field of public administration and public service. Easterly teaches undergraduate political science courses including American government, judicial process, and graduate MPA seminars face-to-face and online.

CPSIA information can be obtained
at www.ICGtesting.com
Printed in the USA
LVHW091457050220
645826LV00009BA/164

9 781498 556088